The Last I.E.P. Book

The ABCs of I.E.P.s

History • Laws • Samples

By Marilyn Arons

Dedication

I dedicate this book to all of the children and their families who have been a part of my life for so many years. In addition, a special "Thank you" to Seth Goldfarb, Jonathan Arons and Nicole Johnson who patiently provided both editing and technical support in the final stages of completion.

The Individualized Education Program (IEP) means a written statement for each child with a disability that is developed, reviewed, and revised in a meeting in which the parents are members of the IEP team. The contents of the IEP are specified at 34 CFR, Part 300.320-300.324 and must be in effect at the beginning of each school year.

TABLE OF CONTENTS

Table of Contents Continued...

The Last IEP Book Continued

But always the surest guarantee of change and growth is the inclusion of living persons in every stage of an activity. Their lives, their experience, and their continuing response- even their resistances- infuse with life any plan which, if living participants are excluded, lies on the drawing board and loses its reality.

Margaret Mead

FORWARD

It was 1977. My daughter, Melody, was nine years old and in special education with multiple disabilities. The local Director of Special Services told me about a new law I should know about and gave me a copy. That was P.L. 94-142, The Education for All Handicapped Children's Act of 1975. Its regulations had just been published. After reading the laws a few times, it was clear to me that this thing called an IEP, Individualized Education Program, was the key for Melody to receive the services she needed. Her school had scheduled an IEP meeting, our first one, and her father and I were invited to come and participate. I had no idea how to write an IEP or what the process was. I called the State and county office of special education to ask how an IEP worked and how I should prepare for the meeting. Nobody explained this to me so I had to teach myself. Though I'd read the law I didn't understand how an IEP was actually developed.

I got every report written about Melody and covered the living room floor with those pages. They were everywhere. One little girl and all that paper! I put a floor length scroll of paper down the middle of the room to write on as I walked around, trying to figure out what the reports meant and what they had in common. I was looking for patterns of her functioning. Finally, I analyzed the strengths and weaknesses from every report and listed them under the columns of Strengths and Weaknesses. That's what I understood the law to require in order to address her specialized needs. As many times as a deficit or strength was mentioned I wrote it down under the headings for Strengths and Weaknesses. I took out all of the extra words and narratives, and focused only on the exact description of her problems. It took days. It was both an emotional experience and a revealing one. Our dog and cat ran through the room, my toddler crawled to find me, and I'd have to reorganize everything again. But her needs finally began to take shape, common patterns running through all of the reports. I did not know what I was doing relative to writing an IEP, but simply tried to better understand what her disability was and how to improve it. Once I was done I typed out my information and comments about what we thought our daughter needed in order to learn. Then came the IEP meeting. I was nervous and did not know what to expect. I gave the group our written input, Melody's information categorized under the headings of strengths and weaknesses. Later on I would reorganize the weakness column into subdivisions and call them Goals. The child study team, my husband, and I discussed Melody's current status, working out areas of disagreement when they arose, and left with an IEP we liked.

I remember Melody's beaming face when looking at the papers covering the living room floor. She was amazed at the many pages having her name on them. "Is it all about me, Mommy?" she asked. "Yes, Honey. It's all about you." Each IEP is "about me". As you work through this book, remember that the job is to create an IEP that looks and sounds like your child. It truly is "about me". Not the school, not you. An IEP is always "about me."

HISTORY

Special education was born in 1975 with the enactment of P.L. 94-142, the Education for All Handicapped Children's Act of 1975. Two years later, the implementing regulations were published. The heart of this broad and sweeping legislation was the commitment to provide specialized instruction to disabled children in order to mitigate the impact of their disability on their education. The key to the provision of a free and appropriate public education for all of America's handicapped children was reflected in a written document called an Individualized Education Program (IEP). This set forth the instruction and support services unique to the individual child and at no cost to the parent. This was a radical and revolutionary law that brought children out of the shadows, and required retraining for every public school employee in the country. Sadly, that training was never provided in the way it was envisioned. There was little money budgeted to fund the requirements of this new law that was to create systemic change at every level of the educational system. There was neither adequate funding nor political will to make it happen. Not only was each disabled student required to receive services, but parents were to be joint and equal participants in all decisions affecting the education of their child. In the same way that professional educators were not sufficiently trained in the IEP provisions, neither were the parents trained in their role. Most were and remain unaware of either their rights or their responsibilities under P.L. 94-142, "The Act".

By 1979, it was abundantly clear that implementation of this powerful and highly regulated system of special education was in deep trouble. At that time, Research for Better Schools, Inc. published four volumes on special education, funded under contract with the Bureau of Education for the Handicapped, U.S. Office of Education, Department of Health, Education, and Welfare. They were called "Exploring Issues in the Implementation of P.L. 94-142". Central to these issues was the process and written product of the individualized education program, the IEP. It was viewed as a "change agent" in the country's public school system. Unfortunately, none of the findings or recommendations within these four volumes was ever implemented, in the same way that the system of special education envisioned in 1975 was never implemented.

In 1980 Ronald Reagan was elected President. His administration took on entitlement programs in general, and special education in particular. As a result of that focus and continued lack of special education funding, its demise was assured. Monitoring and federal oversight greatly diminished, and only paper compliance occurred. By 1989, the philosophy of Inclusion permeated every facet of special education. Inclusion dictated that regular education placement was a civil right, the disabled child to be automatically placed there with special services brought into that classroom. Parents were told that regular class placement was the least restrictive environment, with nothing said by the school concerning the requirement to complete the IEP before any placement consideration. Neither parent nor school staff was

2

informed about the legal mandates requiring no placement consideration until after specialized instruction and related services were determined.

In 1982 came the Rowley decision (Hendrick Hudson Dist. BOE v. Rowley, 458 U.S. 176). The U.S. Supreme Court held that a disabled student was not entitled to the "best" education, but only that which was appropriate and provided "some benefit" as shown on the IEP. Rowley's impact led several states to conclude that as long as the disabled student got "some" benefit from special education, that was enough to satisfy the legal requirement. No further mention of IEPs at the federal level occurred until 1992. The federal government published a comprehensive series of "Questions and Answers" about the IEP, what it was, who was to participate, and what was to be placed in the written document. That remains the only federal guidance provided on IEPs to date and appears in its entirety (with the exception of legal citations) at the end of this book.

Federal and State monitoring of IEPs over time became extremely lax, and no state was punished for violating P.L. 94-142 (and all of them did in one way or another). A state could be found in compliance by the federal government when none of its IEPs conformed to federal requirements and when parents were not welcomed into IEP meetings as equal participants. The inequity displayed toward parents at IEP meetings gave rise to the growth and use of advocates, consultants, and nonlawyer representatives who often accompanied parents to these meetings.

Over time, due to the escalating costs of special education, tremendous effort was made across the nation to lower the number of children who were referred to child study teams for evaluation. Groups of students, labeled as having a "Specific Learning Disability", were particularly targeted. Some states put a cap on the number of students who could be referred to special education and who could be found eligible to receive special education and related services. Inclusion spawned hundreds of federally funded groups who supported only general education placements and who did not provide parents with the right to a continuum of placement options beyond that of the regular classroom. By the 1990s and into the 21st century, Inclusion split into two streams. One was called Response to Intervention (RTI). This used a variety of interventions to prevent referral to special education and to help the child through general education services. After 20 years, research has shown the use of RTI to have been questionable. It did not achieve its intended goal and was abused by creating more difficulty for children's referral for special education evaluations and eligibility determinations. The second stream, called "Universal Design", was created through the reauthorization of P.L. 94-142 in 2004. This philosophy said that a regular classroom should dumb down its curriculum and program requirements so a broader group of learners could receive instruction together, achieving "some benefit". Consistently, the political and educational goal has been to

(1) decrease the numbers of students in special education, especially those with invisible learning disabilities, and (2) to deprive their parents of the procedural safeguards guaranteed when their children were eligible for special education.

Special education has become big business. As school budgets declined, special education continued to demand individualized services, often at the expense of general education. School board attorneys, and a few lawyers specializing in helping parents of disabled children, began to intervene and to participate in IEP meetings, making them adversarial and overly legalistic. School systems became overloaded in every way, with difficulties in funding and in keeping talented staff that were skilled at working with both disabled children as well as their parents. More and more special education teachers left the profession due to the pressure of litigation and the amount of paperwork that schools required. Computerized IEPs were used exclusively, containing many pages that had nothing to do with the individual child and with little actual information about the necessary specialized instruction that was needed. Schools were afraid to be specific in any aspect of the IEP because of the fear that they would be sued if instruction was too specific and not implemented. As a result, by 2017 the development of IEPs is largely governed by the school board attorney or his/her designee, particularly if a parent is seen as a threat to the child study team or to the district.

Special education is 42 years old, entering middle age; yet, it is still the infant, trying to develop into a fully grown adult of service delivery. I have been the parent of a child with special needs, a special educator, an advocate and a nonlawyer who has worked every day in special education throughout these 42 years. The contents of this book reflect this work in these various capacities. All of the IEPs, one for each category of disability, are those that I wrote for real children in actual cases. None are perfect. Each one is different from the other. Some were written at a judge's directive because the school district did not know how to develop an IEP from scratch, relying only on their computer generated IEP banks. The law was renamed in 1990, now called the Individuals with Disabilities Education Act. That new name did not fix IEP problems.

All involved with special education took a long time to get there. Mothers took nine months to give birth and mothers and fathers raised their children over many years. It took time. Teachers, administrators and therapists have spent years in school and in passing licensing exams. It took time. To learn something that is new takes time and practice. Learning to write a truly individualized IEP takes time. Put in that time. Enjoy the challenge and learn more about the child. Be patient. Know that there is more than one right way to do something. Learning to write an IEP takes less time and money than participating in a trial. Both school and parent should put their resources into programs and services and not into litigation.

Endrew in 2017

2017 is the year that the United States Supreme Court clarified what an IEP is in the Endrew F. v. Douglas School Dist., March 22, 2017 opinion. It said:

The essential function of an IEP is to set out a plan for pursuing academic and functional advancement...the degree of the progress contemplated by the IEP must be appropriate in light of the child's circumstances...that child's educational program must be appropriately ambitious in light of his circumstances. The Act contemplates that this fact-intensive exercise will be informed not only by the expertise of school officials, but also with the input of the child's parents or guardians. The goals may differ, but every child should have the chance to meet challenging objectives. The IEP is the centerpiece of (IDEA's) education delivery system for disabled children.

The adequacy of a given IEP turns on the unique circumstances of the child for whom it was created. The nature of the IEP process ensures that parents and school representatives will fully air their respective opinions on the degree of the progress a child's IEP should pursue; this, by the time any dispute reaches court, school authorities will have had the chance to bring their expertise and judgment to bear on areas of disagreement. A focus on the particular child is at the core of IDEA. The nature of the IEP process, from the initial consultation through state administrative proceedings, ensures that parents and school representatives will fully air their respective opinions on the degree of progress a child's IEP should pursue.

Every IEP includes "a statement of the child's present levels of academic achievement and functional performance", describe(s) "how the child's disability affects the child's involvement and progress in the general education curriculum", and set(s) out "measureable annual goals, including academic and functional goals, along with a "descriptions of how the child's progress toward meeting" those goals will be gauged. The goals may differ, but every child should have the chance to meet challenging objectives. The IEP must also describe "special education and related services...that will be provided" so that the child may "advance appropriately toward attaining the annual goals: and, when possible "be involved in and make progress in the general education curriculum." An IEP is not a form document. It is constructed only after careful consideration of the child's present levels of achievement, disability, and potential for growth. The adequacy of a given IEP turns on the unique circumstances of the child for whom it was created.

Endrew established new standards for the contents of the IEP in that its contents must be appropriately ambitious, fact sensitive, and focus only on the particular child. Endrew requirements are:

1. The child's circumstances determine whether or not the contents of the IEP are appropriate.

2. IEPs are fact sensitive.

3. Every child must have the chance to meet challenging objectives.

4. Parents and school are to fully air their opinions at the IEP meeting.

5. Focus on the individual child is at the heart of special education.

6. The IEP must describe the special education and related services to be provided.

7. An IEP is not a form document.

8. The degree of progress projected in the IEP must be appropriate in light of the child's circumstances.

Endrew renews the focus on genuine, individually designed instruction for disabled students. It cannot be instruction that comes from a computer bank and looks like that of other students in a particular class. Schools, over time, have been loath to examine subtest scores on their standardized test results. Yet fact intensive data can only come from examination of all data, with particular emphasis on considering the gap between strengths and weaknesses. Age norms, grade norms and averages are to be discouraged in that they blur the discreet areas that require special education. Percentile scores are always preferred.

Currently IEPs are designed by schools so that the school doesn't fail. Goals and objectives are frequently put in the document that the child already knows. Instead, challenging objectives that intensively work on deficit areas are required by Endrew. IEP meetings have evolved to the point that no opinions are fully aired. The school staff are afraid that whatever they say will be twisted and that they may have to testify at a hearing. Parents are often mute and agree to anything the school suggests, or come in with experts and advocates to intimidate the school into giving them what they think their child needs. It is rare now that opinions are fully presented with differences explored and resolved. IEP discussions often try to emphasize the wide range of normal and to minimize the degree of impairment. Schools often point to how the student performed on group tests, and frequently fail to examine the internal strengths and weaknesses of the child apart from the group. No school uses bona fide evaluation criteria. Endrew provides renewed hope for systemic change and the ability of parents and school to develop legitimate IEPs.

IEP FLOW CHART

Comprehensive_____ Evaluations

Educational   Medical   Social   Psychological   Functional   Other

Current _____Status

*Description of disability's impact   *Written in measureable terms   *Direct relationship to
on academic/nonacademic areas   goals, objectives

_____Goals_____

These are measureable, instructional statements made to describe expected
growth over 12 month period

Instructional_____ Objectives

These are a logical breakdown of the major subdivisions of the goals, serving as
milestones for their measurement.

Transition Goals and Objectives by age 16

Transition is aimed at independence, post- secondary education, and/or
employment after graduation.

Related_____Services

These are corrective or supportive services that include, but are not limited to
transportation, developmental, and functional services that are provided in
addition to the educational program.

Named Placement

The placement for the child must be specified in the IEP, as well as the rationale
for that placement choice based upon implementation of the IEP.

GETTING READY

This book is designed with a particular focus on parents. However, its use should equally benefit child study teams, as well as teaching and support staff in both general and special education. How do you prepare for an IEP meeting?

KNOCK, KNOCK. WHO'S THERE?

In order to collect your fact intensive information about the child, ask and answer the following six questions.

1. *WHO IS YOUR CHILD?* Before the IEP meeting, write a description of your child, and include all strengths and weaknesses. Describe the level of independence in all areas of daily living, homework completion, and social skills. Look at the IEP currently being implemented. Go through the goal headings and ask your child, when possible, what the teacher did in the goal areas listed. I often suggest that the parent go one day without helping or interfering with the child's play or work at home, mindful of safety. Carefully observe. What does your child do independently, enjoy, avoid. Do not help. Just watch and record.

2. *WHO IS YOUR CHILD'S TEACHER?* Meet with your child's teacher before the IEP meeting. Ask about areas of strength, weaknesses, participation in any basic skills programs, other remedial or enrichment programs, social skills, organizational skills, peer interaction in class and during play, involvement of the school nurse or guidance counselor, and the concerns and viewpoint of the teacher. This provides parents with a different viewpoint about the child, and also gives them information about the teacher.

3. *WHO ARE YOUR CHILD'S OUTSIDE- OF- SCHOOL ADULT FIGURES?* Speak with anyone outside of school who knows your child. These include teachers or friends involved with sports, music, art, church, tutors, parents of other school children, doctors, neighbors, extended family. What is their input about your child's status?

4. *WHO ARE THE CHILD'S PARENTS?* Genetics plays a large role in understanding the child, particularly with certain disabilities. Did the parents have problems similar to the child? Are the parental concerns reasonable? Are they in denial about the disability? Who takes care of the child when he/she is not in school? Does the family understand the ramifications of their child's disability?

5. *WHO HAS YOUR CHILD'S SCHOOL RECORDS?* Make an appointment to look at all of the school's records about your child. They are supposed to be kept in one place, but are actually in several departments (special education, principal, teacher) and with a variety of school personnel. You are entitled to copies of all of them and will be surprised to see how many of

them there are. Read the current records and look at the levels of functioning in academic, social and emotional areas.

6. *WHO IS IN CHARGE OF THE REGULAR EDUCATION CURRICULUM?* Usually this is the school building principal. Find out what is taught in regular education for the upcoming grade for the child. Look at his/her current levels of functioning. Match them with what is required in regular education. If there is a significant discrepancy, the specialized instruction in the IEP begins at your child's current levels of functioning, regardless of what the regular education curriculum is.

You must prepare for the IEP meeting with the same amount of effort you put into your job or home. Special education is a joint endeavor between the school and the family, both having equal but different responsibilities. Participating in the IEP meeting means that you have the information you need in order to give your opinion about the instruction and services needed for the upcoming school year. Once you do the ground work, you become better organized each successive year. Less preparation time is needed once you understand how to gather and interpret the academic and functional information about the child. The journey into special education becomes easier when the preparation becomes routine. It is vital to understand that your participation in the IEP process is a contract negotiation for services. It specifies the specific instruction for the child, as well as the corrective or supportive services needed to benefit from special education. You cannot sue if the child does not achieve the projected yearly growth on the IEP because it is not a performance contract. But it is a contract for service delivery. Read every word of the present or proposed IEP. Was it implemented? If not, why not? If yes, how much measureable progress did the child make in all areas of specialized instruction? This becomes part of the intensive fact finding in preparation for the following school year.

ATTITUDE

It is natural to be anxious about the child's IEP meeting. It is also common to be upset or angry about a certain situation or event. There are times when a school employee may say or do something that upsets you. You may also upset a staff member by what you say or do. Remember that this meeting is about identifying the fact specific needs and strengths of the individual child and not about the personal animus of the adults toward each other. There should be no name calling, raised voices, or temper tantrums. It is highly recommended that the parent submit their ideas for the IEP in writing before the meeting so that the school knows what is wanted and why. Tape record the meeting, holding both parent(s) and school accountable for what is said and done. Give advance notice so that the school can also make a recording, which becomes a pupil record. Be extremely polite. Learn to listen, take notes, and wait your turn to speak. Remember that how you look and the expression on your face says as much as the words used. Power phrases to use during the meeting include:

I hear you.

I hear you but respectfully disagree.

We can agree to disagree.

Gentlemen of good will can differ.

What a good idea.

Thank you for explaining that.

Do not be afraid to ask questions or have the test data explained in words you understand. Be prepared to answer questions. If you believe they are too personal or asked in bad faith, you have the right not to answer. However, every effort must be made for full disclosure and to find areas of agreement, making it easier to resolve disagreements.

CLASSIFICATIONS

The child receives an IEP when he/she is found eligible to receive special education and related services. This eligibility is a federal entitlement for the child to receive a free and appropriate education from the public school district when diagnostic and functional information matches one of the thirteen categories of disability. The parent is not to pay for any service found in the IEP. It is important for everyone involved with the child to agree on the classification because it drives the focus of the specialized instruction. School districts often say that the classification doesn't matter. It does matter, especially if a case is litigated. The majority of disabled children have multiple disabilities. However, when facts cluster around one of the disability categories, it becomes the primary area for specialized services. When disabilities are so intertwined and equal that you cannot separate one from the other, then the child is legally classified as Multiply Handicapped. All deficits, however, that fall outside of the classification must also be reflected in goals and objectives. IEP contents should reflect the specific aspects of the disability which arise under the classification, whatever it may be. Those classifications are:

1. <u>Autism</u>- This is a developmental disability significantly impairing (1) verbal; (2) nonverbal communication and social interaction, generally seen before age 3, that interferes with educational performance. Other characteristics may include: repetitive behaviors, stereotyped movements, resistance to environmental or daily routine change, and unusual responses to sensory experiences.

IEP Considerations for Autism

No consideration of methodology is to appear in the IEP. There are a variety of therapeutic and behavioral viewpoints on appropriate instruction, but these are not to control the IEP contents. No State or organizational philosophy about the number of hours certain services are to be provided can be required. Only the recommendations from evaluations can be used. Instructional areas may include:

1. Verbal communication- No prepackaged program for autism is to be used for the individual child. All autistic children are different. Developmental, functional, academic and medical information is to be used. In addition, oral motor and language problems should also be considered.

2. Nonverbal communication- This involves reading body language, gestures, and tone of voice. Instruction should include predictable ways for the child to convey fear, frustration, happiness, excitement and having to go to the bathroom.

3. Repetitive behaviors- Goals and objectives are required so as to lessen these behaviors which must be named and quantified in the IEP.

4. Unusual responses to sensory experiences- These unusual and predictable responses must be described in the IEP regardless of what it is. Then specific instruction is developed to decrease specific and unusual sensory responses. No methodology used by the school can limit the specificity of the problem to be addressed in the IEP.

5. Stereotyped movements- Goals are required to name and decrease specific stereotyped movements, as well as the behavior used to replace it.

6. Resistance to environmental or daily routine- Name the specific resistance in the IEP, as well as what the child will learn to decrease that resistance. Often, expressive language is used to substitute for the behavior.

....

2. <u>Deaf- blindness</u>- This classification has concomitant hearing and visual impairments, a combination causing severe communication and other developmental and educational problems so that they cannot be met in a program solely for the deaf or blind.

IEP Considerations

A. Severe communication needs- Goals must specify the precise nature of the communication impairment and project the expected progress of the child by the end of the school year.

B. Developmental problems- Goals must be written for any specified problems in the data, ranging from self-care, feeding and toileting to basic initiation and social skills, to more advanced development. Instruction must be designed to decrease the gap between the current developmental level and where the child can be expected to be at the end of the school year with appropriate instruction.

C. Educational problems- These relate to academic skills and how they generalize into the natural environment.

D. Simultaneous programming for both deafness and blindness must be provided. Both are of equal instructional importance and must be integrated simultaneously into the instructional program. (Note: This is also the language used for Multiply Handicapped classification and its required programming through the IEP.)

....

3. <u>Deafness</u>- This is a hearing impairment, whether permanent or fluctuating, that adversely affects a child's educational performance.

IEP Considerations

A. The IEP must state whether this disability is a permanent hearing impairment or a fluctuating hearing loss.

  1. Permanent hearing loss must specify what the child hears with and without amplification. Goals are required to be designed to address all of the deficit areas, such as speech and language, social needs, self-image, and self-esteem.

  2. Fluctuating hearing loss must be described and quantified. Instruction is required to decrease the impact of the hearing loss educationally, socially, emotionally, and in the outside world beyond the school door.

....

4. <u>Emotional Disturbance</u>- This condition shows one or more of the characteristics listed above, over a long period of time, and to a marked degree that affects a child's educational performance:

* An instability to learn that cannot be explained by intellectual, sensory or health factors;

* An inability to build or maintain satisfactory interpersonal relationships with peers and teachers;

*Inappropriate types of behaviors or feelings under normal circumstances;

* A general pervasive mood of unhappiness or depression;

* A tendency to develop physical symptoms or fears associated with personal or school problems;

* Diagnostic terms including schizophrenia.

IEP Considerations

A. The IEP must describe the inability to learn, with written goals to teach the student how to change the behaviors in order to learn;

B. The IEP is required to provide specific, quantifiable instruction to build satisfactory interpersonal relationships with peers and teachers based upon the evaluation data;

C. Inappropriate types of behaviors must be specified, with written goals to teach specific appropriate behaviors;

D. Specifics of the unhappiness or depression must be described, as well as the cause, and what the child will learn to improve his/her present status in quantifiable terms.

E. Describe the personal fears and symptoms. Then write goals for specialized instruction to decrease these symptoms.

F. Describe specific school problems and then write goals to decrease those problems and by how much.

G. Describe observable manifestations of the schizophrenia and what the student is to learn to mediate it, such as medical compliance.

....

5. <u>Mental retardation (Cognitive Impairment)</u>- This reflects s general intellectual functioning that is significantly below that of the same age group. There are also deficits in adaptive behavior that are seen during the child's early development and adversely affect educational performance.

IEP Considerations

A. IEP present levels of functioning must contain the number of the IQ (Intelligence Quotient). There are different instructional implications for those who are mildly, moderately or severely retarded. Each of those categories has a specific IQ range. Goals focus on independence and self-sufficiency, as well as academics. All functional and developmental areas of living on a daily basis must be examined for deficits and subsequent instruction. Projected improvement is to be quantified for measurement by the end of the school year.

B. Adaptive behavior may be the most important aspect of IEP development. It is defined as (Grossman, 1983):

> behavior that is effective in meeting the natural and social demands of one's environment. Considerations include the degree to which individuals are able to function and maintain themselves independently, and the degree to which they meet satisfactorily the culturally imposed demands of personal and social responsibility.

C. Required goals are to improve the social demands on the child within various environments, based upon all of the information.

D. IEP contents must specify the degree of independent functioning and the instruction required to improve it.

E. When there is a discrepancy between culturally accepted norms and the child's current functioning, written instruction is to be provided to lessen that discrepancy.

....

6. Multiply Disabled
- This classification refers to two or more impairments, the combination of which causes severe educational problems that cannot be addressed by special education for only one of the impairments.

IEP Considerations

A. The disabilities that merged to create the category of Multiply Handicap must be described.

B. The simultaneous instruction to be provided must be in writing, as well as how much improvement in the goals is to be expected by the end of the school year.

....

7. Orthopedic impairment- Severe orthopedic impairments include clubfoot, absence of a limb(s) Impairments caused by disease include polio and bone tuberculosis, while causes incude cerebral palsy, amputations, fractures or burns.

IEP Considerations

A. The specific orthopedic impairment must be specified, with an explanation as to how it impacts on the student's education, self-image, self-esteem, independence, self-advocacy, social skills, etc.

B. Goals are to teach the student how to adjust to the impairment, as well as goals for therapies. All instruction and therapies are to be measureable, with projected levels of improvement by the end of the year.

C. Assistive technology is to be considered, the goal being self-sufficiency and independence in all activities and functions of life. An aide may not be appropriate under certain circumstances unless that aide is faded as the student improves.

....

8. Other Health Impairment- This classification is commonly used for students with attention deficit disorders, but also includes chronic or acute health problems such as a heart condition, tuberculosis, rheumatic fever, nephritis, asthma, sickle cell anemia, hemophilia, epilepsy, lead poisoning, leukemia and diabetes. Manifestations are having limited strength, vitality or alertness.

IEP Considerations

1. Specify the precise manner in which there is limited strength, vitality, or alertness.

2. Goals must specify instruction to increase the child's strength, vitality or alertness in quantifiable terms.

3. Medical compliance and teaching its importance is a component for specialized instruction.

4. Specific instruction about the disease may be required in order to teach the student how to function independently and healthfully.

....

9. Speech or Language Impairment- This includes a communication disorder, such as stuttering, impaired articulation, language impairment, and a voice impairment that adversely affects the child's education.

IEP Considerations

1. Specify the stuttering problems and how it impacts upon the child's functioning, including socially and emotionally.

2. Articulation impairments must be documented in evaluations. Quantifiable improvement must be projected by the end of the school year.

3. Specificity of the language impairment must be contained in the IEP with baseline functioning included. Goals are written to instruct the child to improve in measureable terms.

4. A description of the voice impairment and its impact on classroom functioning, and social and emotional development must be provided in quantifiable terms that lessen or compensates for the vocal impairment.

10. <u>Traumatic Brain Injury</u>- This is caused by an external force that results in total or partial disability, psychosocial impairment or both which adversely affects educational performance. The term applies to open and closed head injuries that impair one or more of the following areas: cognition, language, memory, attention, reasoning, abstract thinking, judgment, problem-solving, sensory, perceptual or motor abilities, psychosocial behavior, physical functions, information processing, and speech.

IEP Considerations

A. Complete medical, neurological or related information must specify the nature of the injury and whether or not function can be regained. This is required information so as to determine whether the IEP is to be remedial (the problem can be fixed or improved) or compensatory (teaching the child how to adapt or circumvent problems caused by the injury).

B. Every aspect of the category definition is to be converted into specific areas of instruction based upon the data. This includes: cognition, language, memory, psychosocial, attention, reasoning, abstract thinking, physical functions, judgment, problem solving, sensory, information processing, perception, motor abilities, and speech.

11. <u>Visual Impairment including Blindness</u>- This is an impairment in vision that, even with correction, adversely affects the child's educational performance.

IEP Considerations

A. The kind of visual impairment must be specified and how that impacts upon the educational, emotional, and social life of the child.

B. Quantifiable instruction is required so as to lessen the impact of the disability by the end of the school year.

....

12. <u>Specific Learning Disability</u>- (Note: This represents approximately half of all children in special education. It is also the most misunderstood category of disability because it is seen as less serious than the other categories. As an invisible handicap, its impact upon learning may be grossly understated.)- This is a disorder in one or more of the basic psychological processes involved in understanding or using language, spoken or written, that may show itself in an imperfect ability to listen, think, speak, write, spell, or to do mathematical calculations, including conditions such as perceptual disabilities, brain injury, minimal brain dysfunction, dyslexia and developmental aphasia.

IEP Considerations

1. The IEP team must specify which specific disability the child has. Though a diagnosis cannot be required to appear in the IEP, the name of the learning disability is to be "specific". The exact instructional needs are to be reflected in the evaluations and other data, such as early intervening services.

2. The exact learning disability must be targeted in the IEP, instruction designed to measurably improve the disorder by the end of the school year. A school refusal to use the term "dyslexia" is tied to the methodology and expense of implementing such a program, though these factors are legally not allowed as a consideration. However, in the real world money and staff hold the keys to what the school agrees to put into the IEP.

3. School staff often accuses the child's lack of motivation to explain difficulties in their education. Blaming the child or the family for not responding to education is not permitted. Motivation is not a legal factor in writing the IEP.

4. Affective, or emotional and social issues frequently appear in children with learning disabilities and must be addressed through specialized instruction.

5. The IEP cannot be a computer-generated document from the school's computer bank of goals and objectives. These are to be individually designed to address specific academic, social and emotional needs of the child with quantifiable growth at the end of each school year.

6. Developmental factors must be considered in writing an IEP for a child with a learning disability. They include:

A. Is the age of the child such that remediation is no longer a viable instructional goal?

B. Has the child learned unacceptable coping mechanisms that do mot make him/her available for learning? If so, these must be addressed within the goals of the IEP. The student can never be blamed for the disability, nor given instruction that does not consider the impact of the disability functionally, developmentally or academically.

C. The more intelligent and creative a disabled child is, the more difficult it is to write and implement the IEP. Data must describe how the child learns, including descriptions of giftedness. This information should be compared with the state's curriculum standards by grade in order to examine if it is below the current levels of academic functioning of the child. The need of the student trumps state standards through the concept of "alternate proficiencies".

....

13. Preschool Disabled- This is a child with a disability from ages 3-5. At age 5, the child is eligible for classification. Developmental delay is shown through evaluations performed by the school district. This age group does not have a specific category beyond that of Preschool Disabled, though eleven of the categories of disability provide the template for eligibility. The category not to be considered is Specific Learning Disability. Preschoolers are not entitled to a free appropriate public education because they are not old enough to be in an academic program. Their IEP is called an Individualized Family Service Plan.

....

IEP MEETING PARTICIPANTS

Both the school district and the parents can bring anyone they wish to the IEP meeting as long as that person has information to share about the child. The only caveat regards an attorney. If the parents bring a lawyer, the school must also bring the school attorney. When parents bring an outside expert on their child, the school may decide to also bring the school attorney. The school is to provide a multidisciplinary team of licensed staff with direct and first-hand information about the child. This should include an understanding of the child's intelligence and adaptive behavior, academic levels, social and emotional functioning, strengths, weaknesses, knowledge of the specific disability, and how the child learns. A regular educator may also be present so as to give input about the regular education curriculum and the peer group in a particular grade or class. There must also be a person present who can commit to spending school resources on IEP implementation. Each side should provide notice as to who will attend the meeting.

HOMEWORK

Do you do your child's homework? Do you have to teach the skills to your child that the homework reflects? Are you and your child afraid that if you don't do the homework for them, in full or in part, they will fail the subject? Does the school tell you how well your child is doing when you know the grade is actually a measurement of your work? Stop. Stop doing the homework for your child. Homework is a practice of generalization and drill, a reinforcement of classroom instruction. There is no way for the teacher to know if your child understands the work if you do it. That is a false measurement. If the child is unable to do the assignment, write a note on the paper and explain the problem to the teacher. That is a data point. Include how homework is to be handled in the IEP relative to completion. The parent's job is to support and reinforce, providing a place to do the homework. It is not to teach the skill. Be prepared to discuss this at the IEP meeting if it is a concern.

DISCIPLINE

We are living in a time when school discipline is a one size fits all. Has your child been suspended frequently? Put in time out? Sent to the principal? Have you been called at work to come and pick up your child due to a behavior problem? Discipline is an important component of IEP development for a large percentage of special education students. There is major resistance from school districts to modify school discipline rules so as to assure safety of other students, staff, and the child in question. Discipline is important for the shy child as well as an aggressive one. Think of behavior as language. What does it communicate about the child's wants and needs? Are certain behaviors a part of the child's disability? To prepare for this discussion at the IEP meeting, get a copy of the school's Student Handbook. Ask a professional what kinds of behaviors result from your child's disability. Give your opinion. The Handbook should contain a list of the behavior and conduct rules that are required while attending school. Check those that you think your child cannot meet all of the time. Develop alternate behaviors your child can do or be taught to do to replace those in the School Handbook. Behavior is age related, disability related, and environmentally related. Examine any difficulties within those three areas that may exist and insist specialized instruction be provided in the problem areas.

SOCIAL SKILLS

Schools are notorious for refusing to provide social skills instruction. Social skills are a developmental and functional skill that may require specialized instruction through the IEP goals and objectives. Does the child have friends? Is he/she invited to birthday parties or other out of school events? Does he/she know how to initiate play with another child? Do they have the necessary language skills? Do they have sensory issues that interfere with play? Many educators view social skills as more important than academic skills, so that the parent is not wrong to request instruction in this area. However, the school cannot demand social engagement from one child to meet the needs of another. Inquire as to any extra- curricular activity where your child shares common interests or skills with other children. This is an area in which the family role is crucial. There should be agreement between the social skills taught at school and how those skills are carried over into the home and community.

SOCIAL MEDIA

Cell phones and social media are now part of the daily life of American students, including those with disabilities. The Internet is a key instructional tool in many classes and subjects. What role do social media play in the life of the child? Is specialized instruction necessary in order for the student to use and benefit from this cyber world? The use of and impact from social media needs to be considered in IEP development, particularly for those students with judgment issues, cognitive impairments, and emotional instability.

HOW TO WRITE GOALS

The last section of this book provides many examples of how goals are created. The concept of a goal is to find a common category of instruction under which diagnostic data with common information is grouped. Each list will have discreet information from all areas of testing and observation. For example, decoding refers to the ability to sound out the letters of the alphabet and their various combinations. One would not use a category of Reading because that is too general. It does not tease out categories of instruction unique to the child. Instead, the category of "Decoding" would be appropriate. The process of data analysis for the child that yields goal statements includes:

1. Make a list of every deficit area in all current documents describing the child's functioning, with particular attention to the percentile or number score given in testing.

2. Sort that list into two categories: strengths and weaknesses. This covers academic, social, emotional and functional skills. Take only the highest and lowest numbers from the testing. Leave out all of those numbers in the middle.

3. Sort the high scores under strengths and low scores under weaknesses. All goals will come from the Weakness list. Sort that list into what the deficits have in common through the development of categories.

4. The goal statements come from the categories made by organizing the weaknesses into common themes.

HOW TO WRITE OBJECTIVES

Writing objectives for each goal is much more difficult than developing the goal statement. Every item on the list of deficits under each category of weakness is turned into an instructional objective. Though the law only refers to the requirement for measurement for the goal statements, it is wise to put measurement of achievement after each objective as well. In organizing the objectives, start with what needs to be learned first, second, third, etc. Put them in sequential order of introduction and mastery. In order to understand the development of objectives, one needs to understand Task Analysis.

Task Analysis

Task analysis is a sequential ladder of mastery, from the initial skill to that stated in the goal. It is the act of breaking down complex skills into a behavioral chain with subskills and behaviors. Each part of that chain is stated in its order of biological and academic mastery, functional steps going from the bottom to the top. If any rung of that ladder is skipped or missed, getting to the top is increasingly difficult. Remember that:

1. Task analysis will be different for every child when developing the IEP. Each student starts with a different baseline, with different combinations of strengths, weaknesses, developmental delays, language impairments, temperaments, socioeconomic levels and life experiences.

2. Task analysis is used to determine the specific instruction to be written in the IEP by breaking down the deficits listed under the goal statements. It starts with the numerical and functional data in the present levels of functioning. That is the baseline performance at the beginning of the school year. The end point is how far the IEP team projects that the child can go by the end of the school year.

3. Task analysis assumes no aspect of instruction. While it is not as detailed as a lesson plan, it must provide the sequential steps needed for completion in order to reach the goal.

4. Task analysis includes only one specific task at a time in clear and unambiguous language.

5. The more disabled the child is, the more detailed the task analysis must be, with more steps needed to climb the ladder to the top.

6. Apply task analysis to making scrambled eggs as a concept builder. It might include:

Crack the egg
Break it open into a bowl
Shake in a little salt
Melt butter in the frying pan
Stir in the egg from the bowl to the pan

Take out of the pan with a spatula
Put on a plate

For some students there could be 50 steps to this task, such as eye-hand coordination, grasp, judgment, concepts of "melt", etc. Each may require intensive instruction at very discrete levels that are more general than found in a lesson plan. For higher functioning children, many steps are assumed and do not require direct instruction.

RELATED SERVICES

Related services are developmental, corrective and other supportive services in addition to specialized instruction. The school district cannot have a policy about how many related services will be given, the therapist-to-student ratio, frequency, duration of session. This determination is made at the IEP meeting based upon the data provided. This term does not include a medical device or one that is surgically implanted. Services include, but are not limited to: transportation, speech-language pathology and audiology services, interpreting services, psychological, physical, or occupational therapy services, recreation, including therapeutic recreation, social work services, school nurse services designed to help a child with a disability to receive the special education reflected in the IEP, counseling services, including rehabilitation counseling, orientation and mobility services, and medical services, except that such medical services shall be for diagnostic and evaluation purposes only, and early identification and assessment of disabling conditions in children. Related services often cost more than the educational program, though theoretically money cannot be considered when developing the IEP. However, the fact is that money is always considered and often the deciding factor on any given dispute. The related services list is not exhaustive and can reflect any developmental, corrective or supportive service required in order to address the educational need of the student. Such items as parent training, staff training, or a 1-1 aide are all related services. The frequency and duration of these services is largely determined by the written recommendations of the therapist who has evaluated and or works with the student.

TRANSITION

The transition portion of the IEP is to be as individually developed as the academic portion. It cannot be a prepackaged computer program that is generic for all classified students age 16 and over. These services are to begin no later than the first IEP in effect when the child turns 16, or younger if determined to be appropriate. It is commonly tied to the beginning of high school or when the student begins to accumulate credits for graduation. Appropriate, measurable post- secondary goals that are based on age appropriate assessments related to training, education, employment, and, where appropriate, independent living skills are required. Transition is to include services needed in order to achieve these goals, including courses of study. The goal for independence is seen in the transfer of legal rights in IEP development at the age of majority. One year before, the IEP must inform the child of those rights. Of all of the areas of potential misunderstanding between school and parent, transition is near the top. Anything which facilitates and instructs the student to become a functioning adult is to be considered, particularly in light of <u>Endrew</u> and the requirement for challenging objectives.

THE IMPORTANCE OF NUMBERS

Every aspect of the IEP is to be measureable so as to know what the student learned and applied by the end of the school year. Measurement requires the use of numbers. Currently schools appear to prefer describing the deficit areas with words rather than measuring them with numbers. Failure to properly measure outcome is the central reason for disputes between school and parent. Numbers provide proof of both ability and disability. There are three categories of numerical testing:

1. Individualized testing- This assesses the student against his/her own strengths and weaknesses and not against a peer group.

2. Standardized testing- This conforms to unvarying rules of both administration and scoring, with scores distributed along the bell curve. This measures the child against a group. Interpretation, however, is not to be compared to the group, but to the individual patterns of behavior and performance.

3. Functional testing- This is subjective observation or testing which is developed without specific written rules for scoring. I call this the "Look and Guess" method. It is only as accurate as the training and experience of the observer.

Every test must provide a scoring sheet that contains both subtests and averages. NEVER use the average score. It hides the deficit areas appearing in the subtest scores that require instruction. Get percentile scores whenever possible. It is the most precise measurement, spread out over 100 points. The numbers say what the numbers say. They can be interpreted within patterns of functioning, but they cannot be dismissed. Virtually every dispute can be solved with the use of numbers, if those numbers are accurate. Schools commonly use words such as average, superior, or poor as a measurement device. Each one correlates to a specific range of numbers. Ask for that numerical range and have those numbers placed in the IEP. Other test scoring uses scaled scores, age norms, and grade norms among others. Any number is a starting point for discussion. The better the number, the more accurate the number, the more individualized the IEP will be.

THE LAWS AND HOW TO USE THEM

IEP REQUIREMENTS FOR AGES 3-21

Requirements for the process and content of the IEP appear in the 2004 reauthorization of the Individuals with Disabilities Education Act, IDEA, (20 U.S.C., Sec. 1414 (d)) and their 2006 regulations (34 C.F.R. 300.324). The only specific guidelines explaining how to write an IEP were published in 1992, "Appendix C- Notice of Interpretation". Due to the difficulty of finding that document, it is attached at the end of this book. The legislative history of IDEA, reflected in Appendix C, supports the specificity required when developing measureable and observable individualized goals and objectives.

IDEA was changed, effective June 30, 2017 so as to conform to the Every Child Succeeds Act of 2015. Those changes include:

- Removal of the language "core curriculum subjects", "highly qualified special education teachers", and "scientifically based research". Many states, however, continue to use the Core Standards as their framework for regular education, leading to a diploma.
- The use of alternate route qualifications for special education teachers that lead to certification.
- The definition of "regular high school diploma" now includes diplomas based on alternate academic standards.
- There is a change in assessing students with significant cognitive disabilities who complete alternative achievement standards.

There is a debate as to whether or not parents, as well as school staff, should know the laws controlling IEP development. Most don't. Laws provide the lesson plan for the development of the IEP, the order in which the process is to take place, the equity between parents and school staff, and what must be contained in the final written product. Mastery of the applicable laws is critical for all who participate in the development of a child's IEP.

THE CHILD IS...

1. To have access to the general education curriculum in order to meet their developmental needs. (You need to know what the general curriculum is so as to match it to the current levels of the child.)
2. To be prepared to lead a productive and independent adult life to the extent possible.
3. Parents are to have meaningful opportunities to participate in the education of their children. (This goes beyond the IEP meetings.)
4. To benefit from other local, State and Federal school improvement efforts.

THE IEP PROCESS INCLUDES...

1. Special education is a service and not a place.

2. Assistive technology is to be used to maximize accessibility (in the general curriculum and social fabric of the school).

3. A free appropriate public education (FAPE) emphasizes special education and related services designed to meet unique needs and to prepare students for further education, employment and independent living. (20 USC 1401, Sec. 601). (It does not emphasize regular education.)

4. An assistive technology device is any item, piece of equipment, or product system, whether acquired commercially, off the shelf, modified or customized, that is used to increase, maintain, or improve functional capabilities of a child with a disability. (Technology is heavily used throughout primary and secondary education, though its efficacy is now being questioned relative to how children learn.)

5. Assistive technology services mean any service that directly assists a child in the selection, acquisition, or use of an assistive technology device. The term includes:

   A. An evaluation of the child's needs, including a functional evaluation in the child's customary environment;
   B. Purchasing, leasing, fitting, customizing, adapting, applying, maintaining, repairing or replacing assistive technology devices;
   C. Coordination with other therapies, interventions and interventions;
   D. Training for the child and where appropriate, the family;
   E. Training/technical assistance for professionals who are substantially involved in the major life functions of the child.

6. A free appropriate public education is provided in conformity with the IEP. (If it is not in the IEP, the service will not be provided.)

THE WRITTEN DOCUMENT MUST CONTAIN...

An IEP is a written statement for each child with a disability that is developed, reviewed and revised in accordance with Sec. 614(d) of IDEA. This requires:

   A. The strengths of the child will be considered;
   B. The concerns of the parents for enhancing the education of their child shall be considered;
   C. The results of the most recent testing shall be considered;
   D. Use of positive behavior interventions and supports and other strategies shall occur;

E. With limited English proficiency, there shall be consideration of the language needs of the child as they relate to the IEP;

F. When a child is blind/visually impaired there shall be provision of instruction in Braille and the use of Braille unless it is not appropriate (testing is needed to make this determination);

G. Consideration of the communication needs of the child shall occur, with opportunities for direct communication with peers and professional personnel in the child's language and communication mode, academic level, and the full range of needs. (Consider deaf children, nonverbal, those with receptive, expressive and oral motor impairments)

H. A statement of the child's present levels of academic achievement is required; (Many examples appear in the IEP Samples portion of this book.)

I. An explanation is provided as to how the child's disability affects involvement and progress in the general education curriculum;

J. For preschool children, there is an explanation as to how the disability affects the child's participation in appropriate activities;

K. For children who take alternative assessments, a description of IEP short term objectives shall include:

1. A statement of measureable annual goals, including academic and functional goals that are designed to:
   a. Meet the child's needs that result from the disability to enable the child to be involved in and make progress in the general education curriculum;
   b. Meet each of the child's other educational needs that result from the disability.

L. There is to be a description of how the child's progress toward meeting the goals and objectives is measured, and when periodic reports will be provided on the child's progress toward meeting the goals and objectives.

M. There is to be a statement of the special education, related services and supplementary aides and services to be provided, based on peer-reviewed research.

N. There is access to participate in extra-curricular and other nonacademic activities.

O. There is to be an explanation of the extent, if any, to which the child will not participate with nondisabled children in the regular class.

P. There is to be a statement of any individual accommodations that are necessary to measure the academic achievements and functional performance on State and local assessments.

Q. A decision will be made about the child taking alternative assessment(s) and what particular alternative assessments are to be used.

R. The projected date for the beginning of the services and modifications shall be in the IEP, and the anticipated frequency, location, and duration of those services.

S. Not later than age 16, the child shall have appropriate measureable postsecondary goals based upon age appropriate transition assessments related to training, education, employment, and where appropriate, independent living skills.

T. Transition services, including courses of study, are to be in the IEP to assist the child in meeting the transition goals.

U. Beginning no later than one year before the child reaches the age of majority under State law, the child shall be informed of his/her rights under IDEA, and that all rights transfer to the child.

V. For a child ages 3-5, the prior Individualized Family Service Plan (IFSP) from Early Intervention shall be considered when developing the IEP.

GOALS AND OBJECTIVES

A goal is a category of instruction that describes and measures what a child is expected to accomplish in a 12 month period. IEP objectives are a logical, measureable breakdown of the goals into specific areas of instruction that lead toward fulfillment of the goal. IEP objectives should be projected over an extended period of time (a school year or semester). Classroom instructional plans are for daily, weekly, or monthly instruction and have details not required in the IEP. Any change in objectives requires a meeting and parental consent.

Measureable academic and functional annual goals, are designed to-

A. Meet the child's needs that result from the child's disability, and enable the child to be involved in and make progress in the general education curriculum;

B. Meet each of the child's other educational needs that result from the child's disability.

A description is required of how the child's progress will be measured toward meeting the annual goals. Periodic progress reports are to measure the child's progress toward meeting the annual goals (such as through the use of quarterly or other periodic reports, concurrent with the issuing of report cards) will be provided.

A statement is to be made of the special education, related services, and supplementary aids and services, (based on peer-reviewed research to the extent practicable), to be provided to the child, or on behalf of the child, and a statement of program modifications or supports for school personnel that will be provided for the child-

A. To advance appropriately toward attaining the goals;
B. Be involved in and make progress in the general curriculum, and to participate in extracurricular and other nonacademic activities;
C. Be educated and participate with other children with disabilities and nondisabled children in the regular class;
D. An explanation of the extent, if any, to which the child will not participate with nondisabled children in the regular class and other activities; and
E. A statement is required of any individual appropriate accommodations that are necessary to measure the academic achievement and functional performance of the child on State and districtwide assessments.

If the IEP team determines that the child shall take an alternative assessment on a particular State or districtwide assessment of student achievement, a statement of why-

A. The child cannot participate in the regular assessment; and
B. The particular alternative assessment selected.

The IEP must contain the projected date for the beginning of the services and modifications described, and the anticipated frequency, location, and duration of those services. When behavior impedes the child's learning or that of others, use of positive behavioral interventions and support is to be considered, as well as other strategies, to address that behavior.

When a child has limited English proficiency, language needs of the child as they relate to the IEP are to be considered. When a child is blind or visually impaired, there is to be provision for instruction in Braille and the use of Braille unless the IEP Team determines otherwise, after evaluating the child's reading and writing skills, needs, and investigates appropriate reading and writing media, including an evaluation of the child's future needs for instruction in Braille or decides Braille is not appropriate.

Communication needs of the child must be considered. When a child is deaf or hard of hearing, consideration of the child's language and communication needs is required, as well as opportunities for direct communication with peers and professional personnel-

A. In the child's language and communication mode;
B. Academic level;

C. Full range of needs, including opportunities for direct instruction in the child's language and communication mode.
D. Consider the child's needs for assistive technology devices and services.

Current diagnostic categories generally summarize a child's symptoms, but often don't tell us enough about the process underlying a child's challenges- how the child takes in, processes, and responds to information from the world. These three aspects of biology lie at the heart of the child's ability to think, feel, and interact. Children with the same label may be more different than they are alike and children with different labels may be more similar than they are different in terms of their underlying profiles.

(Greenspan & Wieder)

IEP WORDS AND WHAT THEY MEAN

The outline below simplifies IEP language which both the parent and school must use when discussing the special needs of the child.

Current Levels of Educational Performance
(These are baselines for projected growth over the next 12 months)

Intellectual functioning* Adaptive behavior* Academic achievement*   Social skills* Language skills* Communication Style* Physical development* Medical status*   Classroom performance*

Goals

Goal headings are specific groupings of instruction for language, reading, arithmetic, attention, etc. They reflect every category of weakness found through testing and observation and identified in the current levels of functioning. Goals project expected outcomes at the end of 12 months in measureable and observable terms. You need to see it to measure it.

Objectives

Objectives are sequential, intermediate steps from the baseline developed to achieve the projected goal. Each goal will commonly have several objectives that are written from the discreet areas found under each goal and are patterns of dysfunction seen throughout analysis of the data.

Measurement

Every goal must have an accurate measurement of progress. This requires a percentage and a cut point, such as 90% mastery of single digit addition, as well as progress reports. When schools put a percentage of achievement in the IEP for goals, they typically use "80% mastery". The question is, "80% of what?" There must be a second number, a cut point, where the percentage and the skill level intersect. That way there can be no confusion about how much the student achieved and at what level.

All other requirements in the IEP flow from the four elements listed above. They include:

1. Participation with nondisabled children;

2. Accommodations (It is important to understand that accommodations are not instruction. They are adjustments in instruction, testing, and the educational setting to facilitate the output of the student. It does not show improvement of the student.)

3. Alternative testing if needed;

4. A behavior plan should be specialized instruction reflected in the goals and objectives. If the behavior arises from other than the disability, the cause must be identified and a positive behavior plan developed.

5. When a student has limited English development, the language needs should be established through consultation with a professional who is from the culture and speaks the native language of the student.

6. When a student is blind or visually impaired, the ability to learn and use Braille must be determined through evaluation.

7. Deaf and hard of hearing children require specialists in their disability in order to develop an appropriate IEP. Issues involve use of sign language, cochlear implants, and lip reading.

8. If assistive technology is to be used, a comprehensive evaluation is required so as to determine the appropriate technology and services for the individual child.

TRANSITION

Beginning no later than when the child is 16, and updated annually, the IEP must have-

A. Appropriate measureable postsecondary goals based upon age appropriate transition assessments related to training, education, employment, and where appropriate, independent living skills;
B. The transition services needed, including courses of study, that are needed to assist the child in reaching those goals;
C. Beginning not later than 1 year before the child reaches the age of majority under State law, a statement is made to reflect that the child has been informed of his/her rights that will transfer to the child upon reaching the age of majority.

Transition services are a coordinated set of activities designed to be results oriented, focused on improving academic and functional achievement, and assist in the student in moving from school to post-school activities. It is based on the individual child's needs, taking into account the child's strengths, preferences, and interests. It includes instruction, related services, community experiences, development of employment and/or post school living objectives, daily living skills as appropriate, and a functional vocational evaluation.

10 COMMON CHARACTERISTICS OF EDUCATIONALLY SOUND IEPS

1. Knowledge and skills to be learned are written in observable language so that they can be accurately measured. Example: Reproduce something exactly; produce a product, etc.

2. Performance is defined, recorded and reliably measured many times before, during and after instruction.

3. Strengths are to be used to remediate weaknesses when possible. This serves to both motivate and reinforce appropriate responses. The potential outcome of achieving the objective is to be linked to the areas of interest and strength. Example: Learning to read helps a child interested in acting to learn a role faster and better. Scripts can be used to teach reading.

4. Assignments must be neither too easy nor too difficult. They must be sufficiently challenging so that their accomplishment is rewarding. The goal is to have learning become of intrinsic worth to the student.

5. Punishment is minimized. Positive, rather than negative, reinforcement is sought.

6. Performing a correct answer or response once or a few times is insufficient. The student must be able to repeat or find the answer enough times in rapid succession so as to meet demands outside of the classroom.

7. The student is to be helped to find the correct response by identifying or distinguishing its critical features, such as in an object, event, problem, or concept. Help is to be gradually faded so that the student functions independently and as accurately as possible.

8. The student must be taught generalization, or the ability to apply one idea in a variety of ways. Teaching to both sides of the question, and writing IEPs to reflect mental manipulation assists with generalization.

9. Students must actively participate in their instructional activities. Examples: Work with the teacher in setting instructional goals; tutor peers or others, record their own progress.

10. Retention of information is planned and not left to chance. Opportunities are to be provided for ongoing application of the newly learned material in a variety of settings.

(Adapted from Azaroff & Mayer, 1986)

IEP

SAMPLES

The most significant moment in the course of intellectual development, which gives birth to the purely human forms of practical and abstract intelligence, occurs when speech and practical activity, two previously completely independent lines of human development, converge.

(Vygotsky)

IEP SAMPLES

There is no such thing as a perfect IEP. Laws give us the criteria to find and collect the necessary information and to convert that into instruction. What follows are actual IEPs I have written over decades of work with children in special education and in every category of disability (except deaf-blind). They were done in all regions of the country- rich, poor, urban, rural, and suburban. None of them are perfect. But you do the best you can with what you have in the school records, and then work to get information you need and do not have. This is done through additional testing and often involvement of an outside expert. It is not uncommon now to find IEPs with no numbers in them. Less and less testing is done and the job of writing the IEP is often left to the classroom teacher alone. In that I have been in special education since it started in 1975, I can vouch for the fact that no training has been given to teachers with the specifics found in this book. IEPs are less and less prescriptive so that the school district can avoid litigation when the goals are not met. If the goals and objectives are not specific and measureable, and left open to interpretation, parents always lose a dispute with a school district about program or placement. This is not the fault of the school. It is the fault of a broken system, inadequate parent training, and no accountability except political patronage.

Teaching parents, as well as school staff, to write an IEP from scratch is a daunting undertaking for both. Parents need to know that the IEP is a collaborative process and whatever they write is just their input to the IEP team. It may not find its way into the written document. The school must understand that parent input is a requirement of the IEP process and collaboration, and should use it if the information is true and accurate. Even though the writing of an IEP seems overwhelming, there is a huge pay off at the end. The child will have a vastly improved educational experience and show measureable progress by the end of the school year. School staff does not have the training or the time to write IEPs as now envisioned by Endrew, and envisioned at the outset of P.L. 94-142. Therefore, it is up to parents to push the system into writing IEPs that are actually individualized. It is important to remember that school employees are controlled by a pay check. They may be unable to give the input they want or to support the parent as they want because the school administration forbids it.

Never permit the school to say that a specific objective or related service is not needed in the IEP because the service is done automatically as part of the curriculum. Unless it is in the IEP there is no guarantee that the services will be provided. Even though the IEP meeting may get tense, learn to keep calm and focused. If you prepare properly you will do fine. Your facts cannot be rebutted by the school's opinion. Fact must be met with fact. As your mother told you, be polite no matter what is said or done at the meeting. If you need a break, ask for it. Step outside, cool down, and then go back and continue. Parents are not viewed as experts. Even experts are not viewed as experts when it comes to their child. The school holds a stacked deck unless you know how to prepare and how to conduct yourself when there is a disagreement. School staff has an equally hard job to satisfy their supervisors while also trying to develop instruction to advance the child's progress. Finally, never, ever discuss placement until you write the instructional goals, objectives and related services. Both parents and schools are guilty of this and both try to game the system. Don't. Follow the steps and write a program based exclusively on the factual information.

Examine the IEPs that follow to improve your understanding of the process, as well as how to work through a problem when there is not enough factual data available. There is always an answer and a way to teach the child. The job of the IEP team is to find it. As you examine each IEP presented here, there will be many differences. What they share are clean lists of strengths and weaknesses. That is where you start. Get rid of all the narrative and description, naming only specific areas of weakness and strength. Look for patterns across reports and integrate all of this information. Once you strip away all of the extra words and organize information according to strengths and weaknesses, you determine subheadings that accurately connect the patterns of deficit you found in the reports. The name of the subheading becomes your goal statement. All of the weaknesses listed under that heading become the instructional objectives. Related services support the instruction through therapies, special staffing, equipment, and/or transportation.

If children do poorly in language, people assume they are not very bright or poorly educated, but when they do poorly in the nonverbal rules of interaction, people- especially playmates- see them as "strange", and avoid them. These are the children who don't know how to join a game gracefully, who touch others in ways that make for discomfort rather than camaraderie- in short, who are "off". They are children who have failed to master the silent language of emotion, and who unwittingly send messages that create uneasiness.

(Goleman)

AUTISM

Autism is a developmental disability significantly affecting verbal, nonverbal communication, and social interaction, generally evident before age three, and adversely affects a child's educational performance. Other characteristics are engagement in repetitive activities, stereotyped movements, resistance to environmental change or change in daily routines, and unusual responses to sensory experiences. Because autism is a spectrum disorder, there is an enormously wide range of strengths and weaknesses within this population. Current IEPs for autistic children are often written according to the methodology to be used, such as applied behavior analysis (ABA), sensory integration (Floor time), and eclectic mixes of both. This is an error. The IEP must reflect the precise areas of deficit and current baseline functioning. Goals and objectives are then written, regardless of methodology. Factual information describes the child in a variety of settings and circumstances, methodology becoming evident as a result. I have written hundreds of IEPs for children with autism. No two of them were the same.

IEP 1

C.M., Boy, Age 18

Classification: Autistic
Profound disabilities across all areas
Retardation, language, self-regulation, epilepsy

PRESENT LEVELS OF EDUCATIONAL PERFORMANCE

Strengths	Report	Weaknesses
	Neurological report	

(AE= Age Equivalent; ADL= Activities of Daily Living)

Strengths	Weaknesses
Ability to speak a short sentence	Autistic disorder
Some independent phrases for wants/needs	Seizure events
Relatively neat eater	Awake from 2-5 A.M.
	Goes to school very tired
	Self-injurious behaviors (hand-biting)
	Low frustration tolerance
	Aggressions
	Compulsions
	Impulsivity
	Poor mood regulation
	Disinhibited behavior patterns
	Insatiable appetite
	Open mouth posture
	Regression in bike riding
	Uses mostly single words
	No communicative supports
	Maladaptive behaviors
	1.2 daily self-biting/scratching
	Pinching/item destruction
	1.3 daily inappropriate touching
	4.9 daily aggressions/self-injurious behaviors
	2.4 daily destructive behaviors; danger to himself and others
	Latency of response
	Responds promptly after seizure
	Very poor labile closure
	Slow, slapping walking gait
	Neck flexor weakness
	Reduced truncal tone
	Talked more at home
	Spontaneously aggressive at home
	Bilateral cerumen impacted external ear canal
Tickling elicits more responses	Chronic self-biting

37

Strengths	Weaknesses

Neurological Continued

Strengths	Weaknesses
Personal ADL skills- 4.6 AE	Occasional drooled saliva
	Very sluggish, delayed responses
	Heavily medicated
	Leiter score % ile- <0.1
	Interpersonal relationships-1.6 AE
	Severe mental retardation
	Obesity
	Occluded ear canals
	Adaptive coping deficits
	Communication impairment

....

Speech Report

Strengths	Weaknesses
Interactive video games	Self-stimulating hand movements in all settings
1-2 word utterances for tangible activity	Weak bilabial control
Says phone number independently	Low facial tone
Receptive 1 word Picture Vocabulary- 4.2 AE	Escapes educational setting
Thrives on positive reinforcement	Response to rapid instructional pace/volume
	Sensory integration needs
	His size/strength an issue
	Daily aggression at home
	Open lip posture/tongue sticking out
	No production of multisyllabic words
	Final consonants in a word
	Medial syllables in 3 syllable word
	Low arousal
	Inconsistent yes/no/ what questions
	No generalization of address
	Delayed echolalia phrases
	Eye contact/joint attention

....

Expert report

Strengths	Weaknesses
	Concern about unaddressed seizure activity
	Inappropriate use of ABA methodology
	Unsafe in a car when driving w/ CM
	Parents/brother in serious jeopardy
	No skills for independence/self-sufficiency
	CM is a danger to himself
	Regressed in language/cognition/academic skills
	No generalization of functional skills
	Little ability to initiate/engage with others
	Complete peer isolation

C.M. was unstable medically. His school district and private placement denied he had epilepsy, keeping those reports from the parent. No comprehensive IEP that met the federal requirements could be written until he was properly medicated and monitored on a 24 hour basis. Residential placement was ordered at school expense because his educational and medical needs could not be separated. His placement was to stabilize him, verify his medical status, and develop an educational program to occur 30 days after admission to a residential treatment center. This is an example of using the data you have and letting it speak for itself. The goal is to organize it, in spite of technical terms used, so that the patterns of functioning can be seen. Whenever possible, it is important to learn what the terms mean and how to say them. For the severely autistic, this is a highly complex task with expert help often needed to clarify issues. For many, information gathering is overwhelming. Nonetheless, that information is important to understand in lay terms, so that it can be integrated into the IEP as appropriate. Whenever educational need cannot be separated from educational need, both are viewed as educational in nature.

Action is only instructive when it involves the concrete and spontaneous participation of the child himself with all the tentative gropings and apparent waste of time that such involvement implies. It is absolutely necessary that learners have at their disposal concrete material experiences (and not merely pictures), and that they form their own hypotheses and verify them (or not verify them) themselves through their own manipulations.

(Piaget)

IEP 2

M. M.

(Note: M.M. was high functioning, with severe social and emotional problems and unmet sensory needs. He was articulate about specific topics, experienced rage, and drew pictures of violence and death against his peers and teaching staff.)

Boy, Age 18

Classification: Autistic
Problems with social relationships, self-image,
Uncontrolled rage and academic weaknesses
No Transition Plan

Strengths	Report	Weaknesses
	Psychological	
Makes videos		Executive functioning clinically significant
Works w/electronics/technology		Initiating social contact
On swim team		Working memory
Wants to be film animator		Planning/organization
Meticulous/cooperative 1-1		Organization of materials
Matrix reasoning/Information- SS 11		Functional communication
	Educational	
Friendly/cooperative		Oral language- 4.7 GE (grade equivalent)
Broad written language- 11.0 GE		Understanding directions- 4.2
Brief writing- 12/5 GE		Applied problems- 5.7 GE
Spelling- 13.0 GE		
Reading fluency- 13.0 GE		
	Central Auditory Processing	
Phonemic synthesis		Auditory Sentence Memory- 1%ile
Pitch patterns		Number memory- 10%ile
Random gap dictation		Auditory word memory-2 %ile
		Auditory closure- L ear-borderline
		R ear- Below ave
	Speech Language	
Good w/plot		Using process of elimination
Oral presentation		Comedy/joke telling
Morphological completion- 17.9 AE		Taking in emotional state of others

Strengths	Report	Weaknesses
	Psychiatric	

	Flat affect
	R/O delusional disorder
	"Nobody can help me be happy. Film making is all I want to do."

....

Vocational	

Strengths	Weaknesses
Film making	May not always understand what is said
3D animations	Extra time needed to grasp complex/abstract relationships
High degree of interest in artistic fields	Clerical test time- 5 %ile
Visual information processing	Presents as younger than age
Form Perception – 89%ile	Needs time to process tasks
Works well for tangible goal	Feels nervous when talking to people
Very concerned w/accuracy	Spatial aptitude- 24%ile
Spends significant time rechecking work	
Clerical Perception- 99%ile	
Visual Information Processing- 95%ile	
Immediate/Sequential; Visual Memory- 95%ile	

....

PRESENT LEVELS OF EDUCATIONAL PERFORMANCE

(This is the narrative portion of the IEP where all input, functional, developmental and academic, is presented. It provides baselines for the subsequent goals, objectives, transition, and related services. By putting the data from the reports into telling the story about the child, the IEP team and parent can better understand the disability, how it impacts on the child's life, and how to design special education to advance improvement. Lists make the disability clear. The narrative makes the child a person and tells his/her story.)

Cognition

M.M.'s cognition, measured by the school psychologist, showed his highest scores in Matrix Reasoning and Information, a standard score of 11. IQ testing found him to be in the upper limits of the low average intelligence. Strengths were in recall of factual information, visual processing of information, paying attention to detail, and concentrating and using trial and error methods to solve problems. At the outset, it is important to clarify that there are many forms of intelligence, including creative intelligence. The current psychological data measured academically related areas only, and may not be a true reflection of his actual abilities. His highest scores in verbal comprehension were factual answers to science, geography, literature and history. He had good long term memory for factual information, good verbal comprehension skills, and was intellectually curious. Use of word knowledge is a slight weakness. His lowest score was in use of spatial relations to solve problems. His processing speed through use of visual cues exceeded 50% of his peers. Executive functioning was a weakness. Teachers found him to be a meticulous student who took time to get started on tasks and assignments, and preferred to work alone. In a 1-1 setting, he presented as a sociable person with an interest in computers, film making, and animation. He functioned in the average range in reading and writing, and low average in oral language skills and math.

It is important to interpret his psychological and educational testing through the work of Paul Torrance. He said that IQ tests were an inappropriate way to gauge true intelligence, creativity an integral part of intelligence. Characteristics such as persistence, courage, willingness to take risks, and loving and doing what you do well are important components of cognition. M.M.'s passion for film production, his persistence and courage in continuing to pursue these interests in spite of the lack of school support, and his persistence to keep trying to improve his art as well as his school work show compelling areas of strength. His cognition in areas of strength may be in the superior range when factoring in his recent language scores from educational testing which would lower his IQ score. Therefore M.M.'s cognitive profile reflects a talented and creative student whose scores may be significantly lowered by processing and language deficits, but are not a genuine reflection of his cognition and potential.

Educational Skills

M.M.'s ability to understand verbal directions was a 9.7 AE. This reflected severe auditory processing deficits in sentence memory at 1 % ile, word memory at 2nd % ile, and number memory at 10 % ile. His highest score was in spelling, 23 AE, a concrete visual memory task, and in brief writing at 18.1 AE. His reading and math fluency are average, lowered when he was required to use paper and pencil, though written language scored in the average range. He showed significant growth in speech and language, with increased pragmatic abilities now at the average level. His Central Auditory Processing continues to show severe weaknesses in auditory sentence memory (1 %ile), Auditory word memory (2 %ile), and number memory (10%ile). Algebra 2 presented him with difficulties in a regular classroom, with agreement between family and school to place him in a resource room class for this subject.

Adaptive Functioning

M.M. comes from a long history of sensory integration dysfunction that will remain for the rest of his life. His swimming, music, and sports activities all support his vestibular, proprioceptive, and self-regulation needs. Without such self-regulating activities, including making films and videos, he is often overwhelmed by social, emotional, and academic demands. Within his school day he easily misreads interpersonal situations and communications. He prefers to work alone, an adaptive decision that regulates incoming stimuli and avoids having to take in the emotional state of others. This social isolation, however, makes him angry because he has no friends and believes his needs are not being met. Therefore, a bridge must be formed to gradually connect the work he does alone with the gradual addition of peers who have similar interests. This is shown through his football involvement as a member of the football team, where he made many new friends and gained self-confidence.

M.M. presents as younger than his age, feels nervous when talking to people, and often has a flat affect. He deals with personal and social issues in black and white and sees no shades of gray. He is perfectionistic and meticulous in his work, making every effort not to make mistakes. He wants to help people with their problems and feels rejected without this interactive contact. As a result of surfing the Internet, in combination with his peer isolation, he has learned wide ranging information which he has put together within his personal context of isolation and social unhappiness. Though he usually presents with a friendly face, his recent Face Book posting provides further insight:

Many hope for opportunities, to me it may be my last year. Hey, you never know
what could happen to me or you. After the situations I had from June onward,
I feel it'll never leave my head until it is all-situated out or I may not enjoy another
Christmas again.

M.M.'s school experiences intertwine with his self-image and self-esteem. It is imperative he have a more individualized approach to remedy his isolation through peers who enjoy and understand his passion for film making and production. The psychiatric evaluation reaffirmed the autistic diagnosis and his past thoughts of suicide, recommending individual therapy with follow up by a psychiatrist, and parental monitoring of his Internet use. His periodic discussion of suicide was also shared by a family friend at the IEP meeting. She emphasized the imperative of using a film making program as a way to help him begin friendships through sharing of common interests and experiences. He would benefit from Theory of Mind activities provided through Speech and Language therapy.

Transition

M.M. is highly skilled at film making and in computer technology. This is what he wants to do after graduating from high school and must be codified into his educational transition plan. He is self-taught, but has met with significant success and accolades in non-school projects. With the exception of the building principal, nobody at the school, the CST, or the vocational evaluator has seen M.M.'s film work, have not evaluated it, and are unaware of his technical and artistic skills. He has drawn and written storyboards (comic strips) since approximately age 12. He maintained his own Face Book page using that as a primary vehicle of communication. Attending a film school as part of his individualized program transition needs is an appropriate way to address his transition needs. He appears to have developed pre-production film skills because of his skills making storyboards. He apparently has no experience in working with others on a production staff, which should be a transition goal. While skilled in video shooting and editing, it is unclear whether or not he understands specific language used in film production, such as:

Set up
Cut
Marker
Sound speed
Roll sound
Picture is up

Jobs within the film industry which are realistic upon graduation and post-secondary education include being a production assistant. It is important for him to begin to work as a team member within a film or video group so that he gains real world experience in a field he loves, while developing advanced film and production skills. In addition, these areas of common interests and actions can provide him with his first experience at friendship, reciprocity, and an accepting social environment. Exposure to the film and video industry ranges from such areas as "Image and Sound", to "Computer Animation", to "Film and Video Art", among several other areas.

After graduation, his goal is to be employed in the field of TV production or film, with computers a secondary choice.

He is a very pleasant and cooperative young man who tries to the best of his abilities. He would benefit from actual work experience and learns best through visual processing, which is the modality that film making provides him. It is important to assess if he is able to move between a variety of tasks, his ability to work independently with films already demonstrated. His ability to function independently in social, work, and recreational areas must be addressed. It is important that he have peers with higher skill levels and not those who require supportive employment services. He is 18 and his parents are in the process of obtaining guardianship.

Transition Services

This multiyear plan promotes movement from school to M.M.'s desired post-school goals. His needs, strengths, interests and preferences in each area must be considered, and responsibilities shared among the participants. M.M. will be provided with a program that enrolls him in a film/animation program for half of the day and academics the other half of the day. Bussing will be provided between both components of his school day.

Related Services

Speech therapy will increase focus on Theory of Mind activities, and the ability to read facial expressions and body language. These activities will include generalization into social and interpersonal experiences with the guidance of the language therapist. It is vital that there is integration of these activities into real life, resulting in M.M. not viewing his world in black and white, either/or, but seeing shades of gray through finding success in his areas of strength and respect for his talents and skills.

Community Experiences

M.M. will be provided with actual work experience with other peers in the community who share his interests. When there are opportunities within the school or school activities for him to film or to provide animations, he will be the public presenter of his film.

EDUCATIONAL GOALS AND OBJECTIVES

Transition

Goal: M.M. shall demonstrate the ability to present and have his work critiqued by a film professional.

Objectives:
1. He shall explain the goals of the film, engaging in Q&A with the film professional 100% of the time.
2. He shall accept examination of his film work, and engage the professional in explaining the basis for both positive and negative critique 85 % of the time.
3. He shall demonstrate understanding through dialogue that critique of his work is not a personal criticism, but admiration for his effort and potential 80 % of the time.

Goal: M.M. shall demonstrate conceptual and applied understanding of film image 85 % of the time using the criteria of a film school/professional.

Objectives
1. He shall demonstrate understanding of the rules of film composition.
2. He shall demonstrate and apply the concepts of color theory.
3. He shall demonstrate understanding and application of film lines and shapes.
4. He shall demonstrate understanding and application of directing the eyes of the audience to the next shot.

Goal: M.M. shall demonstrate a basic understanding of the elements of film making 80% of the time.

Objectives:
1. He shall demonstrate understanding and application of film composition, placement of shapes within the frame.
2. He shall demonstrate understanding and application of lighting for film and video production.
3. He shall demonstrate basic understanding of sound design for film and video, recording and manipulating sounds to enhance visual communication.

Goal: M.M. shall initiate friendships with peers in his film class through use of film analysis and examination.

Objectives:
1. He shall examine another student's work with that student, and comment on what he sees and ways that film might be improved or changed 80% of the time.
2. He shall look at facial expressions of his peers and people in the films being shown regarding emotions and what they might be thinking 90% of the time.
3. He shall demonstrate less rigidity to other peoples' viewpoints and accept alternate ideas and projects 75% of the time.

4. He shall demonstrate the ability to accept his mistakes or weaknesses and improve his task completion rate 70% of the time.

Speech-Language

Goal: M.M. shall develop mastery of basic Theory of Mind* concepts and applications 80% of the time.

Objectives:
1. He shall articulate why it is important to show your feelings on your face.
2. He shall pantomime in a mirror the following facial expressions:
   Happy, excited, afraid, shy, angry, sad.
3. He shall articulate how he feels inside when he makes those facial expressions.
4. He shall demonstrate the ability to tell stories about those emotion states.
5. He shall select one (or more) emotion state and draw a story board about that emotion.
6. He shall look at faces in school and in the community and describe what they show him and why.
7. He shall articulate/demonstrate how he can change one feeling in himself into another one through an activity of his choice.
8. He shall demonstrate basic understanding of body language.

Homework completion

Goal: M.M. shall improve his executive functioning 75% of the time.

Objectives:
1. He shall demonstrate the ability to do a task analysis of the assigned homework, so that he can complete it on time.
2. He shall apply his task analysis to complete the homework assignment.
3. He shall gradually limit his rechecking of assignments to no more than two times prior to completion.
4. He will seek out assistance from appropriate staff if he is unable to complete his assignment on time.   **6.**

Related Services

Speech-Language therapy: 1-1, two times per week, 43 minute sessions. This includes time to go into the community for generalization experiences.

Psychological therapy for educational reasons from a mutually acceptable therapist, 1-1, 43 minute sessions, twice per month. It is understood that this therapy is to incorporate Theory of Mind concepts*, address school-based issues only, and decrease concreteness relative to his life options. This therapy must also be mindful of the social and emotional attributes of autism.

*Theory of mind is the ability to know the other person's feelings by understanding body language, facial expressions, tone of voice, etc.

IEP 3

(Note: This IEP shows how to develop categories of instruction from the list of weaknesses in the data. This process is called "chunking".)

G.L., Boy, age 12

Classification: Autistic
Wide academic discrepancies
Deficits in social skills
Sweet, compliant temperament
High IQ

Strengths	Report	Weaknesses
	Educational testing	
Personable	..	Distractible
Sweet disposition	..	Understanding body language
Science, Social Studies- A-	..	Proximity/boundaries
Career Tech- A-		Reading- 2 %ile
Choral Music- Outstanding	Tunes in/out of learning in reading comprehension
Instrumental music- A-		Needs redirection in testing
Math- 86%ile		Long term retrieval- 11 %ile
Sports		Phonemic awareness- 3%ile
Electronic games		Comprehension/knowledge- 1%ile
Working memory- 83%ile		Performing cognitive tasks- <.01%ile
Academic skills- 70%ile		Oral language skills- 8%ile
		Listening comprehension- 4%ile
		Receptive language- 3%ile
		Expressive language- 1%ile
		Paragraph reading- 5%ile
		Main idea
		Literal details
		Inference
		Context clues
		Length of story impacts ability
		Sentence sequence- 16%ile
		Contextual language- 9%ile
		Visual motor integration- 5%ile
		Geometric analogies-<1%ile
		Neurological immaturity/anxiety

Deficit Categories

Reading	Reading Comprehension	Social Skills
Phonemic awareness- 3%ile	Tunes in/out	Body language
Broad reading- 2%ile	Main idea	Proximity
Story length	Literal details	Contextual language- 9 %

Deficit Categories Continued

Listening Comprehension	Written Language	Oral language- 8%ile
Long term retrieval- 11%ile	Sentence sequence- 16%ile	Expressive language- 1%ile
Length of story	VMI- 5%ile	
Contextual language- 9%ile		
Receptive language- 3%ile		

EDUCATIONAL GOALS AND OBJECTIVES

Reading Comprehension

Goal:
G. shall demonstrate conceptual understanding of reading comprehension in texts of appropriate length and reading level.

Objectives:
1. He shall demonstrate the concept that text is the same as a person telling him a story in which he is an active participant 80% of the time.
2. He shall demonstrate understanding of the importance of Title, and that it tells him what to expect in the story.
3. He shall verbally state at least two things the title suggests to him.
4. 4. He shall adjust his reading comprehension by:
   A. Stating if the title is of interest to him and why;
   B. State if the text is fact or fiction and why;
   C. State the time period of the story (past, present, future, century, year, season, etc.)
5. He shall state/write questions he has about the story (who, what, when, where, why, how).

Goal:
G. shall demonstrate grammar/parts of speech mastery as a foundation for his reading comprehension 80% of the time.

Objectives:

1. He shall master identification/use of common/proper noun with 90% accuracy.
2. He shall master identification of pronouns in first, second and third person.
3. He shall master identification/use of all action verbs.
4. He shall master identification/use of all auxiliary verbs: to be, to have, etc.
5. He shall master identification/use of adjectives, applying the three test questions for verification: which, what kind of, how many.
6. He shall master recognition/use of conjunctions.
7. He shall master identification of adverbs, applying test questions for verification: how, when, where).
8. He shall master identification of the subject of the sentence.
9. He shall master identification of the complete predicate of the sentence.

G. shall master reading comprehension a three paragraph story.

Objectives:

1. He shall demonstrate understanding of the concept of "topic sentence" by stating what the paragraph is about with 90% accuracy.
2. He shall demonstrate an understanding that the topic sentence provides the "main idea" of the paragraph, with details provided within the paragraph.
3. Through use of short folk and fairy tales, he shall state the main idea for each. (NOTE: G is a concrete thinker so that his main ideas will be concrete and not abstract.)
4. He shall demonstrate understanding of the term "context", or the words around the main idea with 80% accuracy.
5. He shall identify a "detail" in the paragraph.
6. He shall read the topic sentence and concluding sentence and explain what he thinks happened between the beginning/end of the paragraph with 79% accuracy.
7. He shall identify any word in the paragraph that he cannot read, making a master list of words for later use in decoding and sight word instruction.
8. He shall identify any word in the paragraph for which he does not know the meaning 100% of the time.

Goal: G. shall demonstrate the ability to sequence the events of a story.

Objectives:

1. He shall identify what happened at the beginning, middle, and end of the story with 80% accuracy.
2. He shall demonstrate the ability to create a timeline for the story upon request and/or through self-initiation.

Social Skills

Goal: G. shall demonstrate awareness of proper physical boundaries between himself and others while speaking/playing.

Objectives:

1. He shall demonstrate understanding and application of "arm's length" so that he stands neither too close nor too far away from another person 80% of the time.
2. He shall recognize, interpret, and mimic facial expressions with 70% accuracy.

DEAF-BLINDNESS

This classification refers to concomitant hearing and visual impairments, the combination of which causes such severe communication, developmental, and educational needs that they cannot be accommodated in special education programs only for children with deafness or blindness.

This is the only category of disability for which I've never written an IEP. In doing research to find an IEP example for deaf-blind to put in this book, nothing is on the Internet. So this section has a summary of the elements of a deaf-blind IEP. It provides citations for the locations where more information can be found. The key feature of deaf-blindness is that the combination of losses limits access to both auditory and visual information (National Consortium on Deaf-Blindness, Children Who Are Deaf-Blind, #2, November 2007). The type and severity differs from child to child.

PRESENT LEVELS OF EDUCATIONAL PERFORMANCE

The focus of the IEP must explore and try different communication options and establish a communication system. As the child matures, this system is expanded with increased interaction with friends and classmates. (Mary R. Frey, ED 419 366, Considerations in IEP Development for Children who are Deafblind, 1998) To establish levels of functioning for younger children, the INSITE checklist can be helpful. As the student ages, tools such as MAPS or PATH processes can be used to gather all essential information. The IEP must identify how the child receives information, preferred learning style, and modes of communication to be used. The impact of dual sensory impairments must be recognized, with efforts to promote use of existing hearing and vision while providing appropriate accommodations. This IEP is to be functional, relevant, and age appropriate to the child. Developing language and communication skill is the overall theme. Environmental cues enhance full understanding of various situations regardless of the preferred communication method. Opportunities for repetition and practice of skills across all daily activities are important. Connecting language and literacy through story telling opens up new worlds to deaf-blind children, encourages conversations, and builds language. See (www.pathstoliteracy.org/blog/connecting-language-and-literacy-children,)

Specialized instruction

Instructional areas should consider:

1. Personal needs: feeding, medical, personal hygiene, dressing;
2. Physical needs: special equipment, environmental modifications;
3. Sensory needs: accommodations for vision and hearing needs;
4. Staff/peer education: how to communicate, what behaviors mean)
5. Provision of access and opportunities: extracurricular activities (Huebner, et al, 1995, p. 117)

The IEP must contain information about the child's primary and any secondary disabilities. Services may include:

1. Deaf-Blind Specialist who can provide direct instruction to the child or consultation to staff. He/she understands the unique effects of combined vision and hearing loss in communication, learning, orientation, mobility and social skills.

2. Teacher of Students with Visual Impairments (TVIs) who can help the child use optical (low vision) and non-optical devices (reading stands), identify/modify visual materials (large print), and get materials from the American Printing House for the Blind.

3. Teacher of the Deaf/Hard of hearing who can help with communication and assisted listening devices, and address hearing related literacy issues.

4. Orientation and Mobility Specialist who gives the child skills to understand and navigate the environment, including development of independent travel skills. This specialist must be able to communicate with the child in his/her primary mode of communication such as sign.

5. Intervener is a 1-1 service provider with training and specialized skills in deaf-blindness. He/she facilitates access to environmental information gained through vision and hearing; the development/use of receptive and expressive communication skills; and positive relationships to promote social-emotional well-being.

6. Paraprofessionals are 1-1 instructional aides/assistants who provide support for communication, sensory access, movement, delivery of direct instruction, and personal care for the child. Included in the IEP must be the training needed, how many are used throughout the day and their access to coaching and monitoring by professionals with expertise in deaf-blindness.

7. Interpreters are used if the primary language is sign language. If the child also requires touch/tactile communication, the interpreter must have specialized training in that method. (SPAN, Developing an Effective IEP for Children with Deaf-Blindness: A Parent Mini-Guide, 2011),

DEAFNESS

Deafness means a hearing impairment that is so severe that the child is impaired in processing linguistic information through hearing, with or without amplification, that adversely affects educational performance. This is an extremely difficult area for IEP development due to three different philosophies of instruction for the deaf, as well as awareness of the deaf culture within regular education settings. The three teaching philosophies and methodologies for communication are:

1. Signing, primarily American Sign Language (ASL). ASL emphasizes that deaf children will likely function socially within what is called the "deaf community". Their use of oral language will never be accepted by the hearing world so that they should not be required to use oral language. ASL is a distinct language of its own, with subtle shadings of meaning, syntax, grammar and humor. Instruction is based entirely on the student's increasing ability to sign, a language system used throughout the student's entire educational career. IEPs are written solely around the use of ASL for instruction because it is considered to be the native language.

2. Total communication (TC). This system of teaching is based upon the simultaneous pairing of spoken and signed language throughout all areas of instruction. It permits the student to learn languages of both the hearing and non-hearing communities. TC is more available at primary levels of instruction in public schools through the use of 1-1 aides trained in TC. Secondary programs for the deaf use signing almost exclusively, though public school placements often continue with the 1:1 TC aide.

3. Auditory/Oral. This method teaches no signing. It centers upon the ability to lip read, using oral language in order to function within the hearing world. This is used for those classified as "hearing impaired" because it requires sufficient residual hearing and use of oral language if the child is to benefit from instruction. With the availability of the cochlear implant, the auditory/oral method of instruction is used when needed.

(Note: This IEP uses narrative only, due to the lack of numbers in the student record. In the area of deaf education, methodology comes first, based upon the amount of residual hearing, expert recommendation, and parent preference.)

IEP 1

A.B., Age 7, Girl

Classification: Deaf
Above average intelligence
Good social skills
Auditory/oral method

PRESENT LEVELS OF EDUCATIONAL PERFORMANCE

A has no cognitive deficits and has an at least average IQ. She is extremely deficient in expressive language and needs a hands-on, visually oriented first grade curriculum. Her focus is to be on lip reading, utilizing her residual hearing and visual cues with the instruction of a Teacher for the Deaf. She needs constant redirection and 1:1 assistance in order to stay on task. She becomes mildly disruptive during instruction when she is unable to understand what is being taught. She may take something from another child or get up and go to the bathroom.

A is a bright, sociable child who learns primarily with visual cues. She is extremely adept at discerning what she is to do by scanning the environment and copying from her peers. She lip reads to some extent but does not always focus on the speaker. In a classroom it is necessary to give her 1:1 attention in order for her to understand the material. Her comprehension is largely determined by the material being presented visually. Her ability to deal with visual and hands-on tasks is above average for her age, while her expressive language is very significantly below age expectations due to her deafness.

She has many positive qualities that contribute to her being in a regular class for half of the day where she has made many friends. She plays after school with her classmates, is invited to local birthday parties and other social events where she relates well with her peers. In school her classmates are extremely thoughtful and protective of her. She is an emotionally sturdy and adaptable child who has coped well, though her school program requires movement outside of the school building. She smiles more frequently now than last year and occasionally utters short phrases or sentences.

In an instructional setting she needs constant redirection in order to stay on task. She appears to need to be right with her answers and seeks frequent reassurance. At times she may be unwilling to take an intellectual risk. In decoding, she learns by memorizing sight words. She is presently working in a pre-primer 3 reading book and is estimated to mutter approximately 200 sight words. She does not apply her knowledge of sounds and letters to identify new words. Vowel sounds and final consonant sound/symbol relationships have not been mastered. She requires a visual cue in order to transfer a phonic concept to a new word. She does much better with initial rather than final sounds, many of which are not in her repertoire. A's comprehension skills fall below first grade. She has improved her ability to answer "who" and "what" questions, but comprehension remains on a concrete level. She has difficulty recognizing the main idea of a story and the sequence of events. She is now working on "Where" questions more accurately. Visual aids are consistently used throughout her reading program.

Her oral language is below that of her classmates, but she is improving in her ability to convey a message. She speaks in short phrases/sentences and will make her needs known. Examples of spontaneous speech in the classroom include, "My duck has a boo-boo", or "Dad graduate." She is less hesitant and much more verbal in a small group where she has said, "Rachel, get out W. chair." A. uses telegraphic speech. However, in a large group she is inhibited, but will answer a question. When she speaks about a topic she knows well, she can speak in a complete sentence including a prepositional phrase. In her speech she has mastered all sounds except K and G. All vowels and diphthongs are mastered, while some blends are not. She does a fine job in articulation, but does not carry that over to spontaneous speech or oral reading. She can do opposites from pictures. She has progressed well in controlling her voice in a structured situation, but has difficulty in spontaneous speech. She has particular problems with the "e" sound, where her pitch rises dramatically. Her use of social gestures and memorized speech is much better. She knows at least three nursery rhymes that she recited without visual cues. She communicates much more with both adults and peers.

A's handwriting is satisfactory regarding letter and number formation and spacing. She needs to concentrate on working slower in order to produce neater work. Her written expressive language is below first grade level. While other first graders write sentences, stories and poetry, this material has not been introduced to her because of her limited oral language. In her resource room she will write a simple sentence of 3-4 words from dictation by using her five word spelling list. She cannot construct a written simple sentence independently.

A has not been introduced to spelling in first grade in that she needs to develop her language and decoding skills in order to handle this material. She has been introduced to a weekly five word spelling list but this has not proven to be successful. However, her mother reports that she can spell the words at home.

She is in the lowest math group, and received individual instruction. She has made the greatest progress in this area. Her recall of basic subtraction and addition facts is satisfactory. She knows these facts up to 10. She can add or subtract two digit numbers without regrouping. She works more slowly than her peers. Visual aids introduce every new concept. She has just recently begun to compute to 10 without visual aids. In problem solving, A. is able to handle simple word problems. She has been taught and applies the meaning "are left" and "in all". She has difficulty with "greater then", "less than", money and time. In these areas she is functioning well below her classmates. She has the concepts of: are left, larger, and smaller. She does not understand "greater'. Visual aids are consistently used.

A's science and social studies concepts are well below her grade level. She has begun to show lack of interest since she cannot follow group discussions and interactions. When not involved, she moves around the room. If the lesson lends itself to visual presentation, such as parts of the flower, she becomes much more involved. Her curriculum includes safety rules, seasons, animals, plants and weather. To the extent possible, lessons have been supplemented with visual materials.

In gym, A is on grade level in eye-foot skills, basic movement and coordination. She requires refinement in eye-hand skills, body awareness, physical fitness and skill application. She needs extra work in multiple tasks, concept development and complex tasks. It is to be noted that she has had little to no experience in these activities. She has been under the care of an allergist in order to reduce congestion. She has allergies to molds and a nasal spray has been introduced. She continues mouth breathing and tongue thrusting and may need orthodontic treatment.

In library, A has made amazing strides in understanding what to do and remains present for the group story. She follows with fair attention though she may not understand what is being said. No library work has been introduced at this time.

<u>Deficit Areas</u>

Reading
Math
Communication
Written Expression
Language Arts
Social Studies and Science
Study Skills

EDUCATIONAL GOALS AND OBJECTIVES

<u>Reading</u>

Goal: A will advance one school year in her decoding ability.

Objectives:
1. She will add a minimum of 75 words to her sight vocabulary with 80% accuracy.
2. She will apply phonic skills to decoding words on a mid-first grade level, without visual cues, with 75% accuracy.
3. She will apply phonic skills to decoding words with picture cues on a late first grade level with 75% accuracy.

Goal: A will comprehend written material at the 1.9 grade level with 80% accuracy.

Objectives:
1. She will answer comprehension questions with 75% accuracy that utilize visual cues and are on a mid-first grade level.
2. She will answer comprehension questions with 75% accuracy without visual cues.
3. She will answer comprehension questions based on second grade reading level with visual cues with 75% accuracy.

4. She will answer comprehension questions based on 1.8 reading level material without visual cues by the end of the school year.

Math

Goal: A will be able to independently compute at a mid-second grade level.

Objectives:
1. She shall recall and orally state addition and subtraction facts to 18 with a latency of no more than five seconds 75% of the time.
2. She will increase her speed when computing numbers by 25% with no loss of accuracy.
3. She will shift computations sets from one operation to another without teacher intervention 70% of the time.
4. She will demonstrate mastery of regrouping in simple addition and subtraction problems with 80% accuracy.

Goal: A will demonstrate mastery of early second grade math concepts.

Objectives:
1. She will tell time to the quarter hour with 75% accuracy.
2. She will give the value of pennies, nickels, dimes and quarters with 100% mastery.
3. She will make simple change of $1.00 with 75% accuracy.
4. She will perform basic linear measurement with 75% accuracy

Goal: A will solve math problems independently at a 1.9 grade level.

Objectives:

1. She shall show understanding of the concept "greater than" with 90% accuracy.
2. She will solve problems at a 1.5 grade level with visual cues with 75% accuracy.
3. She will underline in red the key words in problems at mid-first grade level.
4. She will recognize basic problem types that are presented with alternative wording, such as "all together', "the sum of", how many", less than", etc. with 65% accuracy.
5. She will signify understanding of the basic process to be performed (addition/subtraction), carrying it out without visual cues with 75% accuracy.

Communication

Goal: A's mean length of utterance will increase 2 to 3 morphemes per utterance in a 100 word sample.

Objectives:
1. She will consistently use the "s" sound for plurality, third person singular verb ending, and possessiveness with 80% accuracy.
2. She will demonstrate more consistent intonation patterns.
3. She will increase her receptive vocabulary by one year.

4. She will demonstrate understanding of the main idea in simple oral presentations of small group members with 75% accuracy.

Goal: A will communicate verbally with her school peers 70% of the time.

Objectives:
1. She will initiate a simple conversation 70% of the time.
2. She will respond to a classmate's conversation 65% of the time.
3. She will sustain verbal exchanges with a classmate of 4 to 5 utterances.
4. She will focus on a speaker addressing her entire class 75% of the time.
5. She will increase the frequency with which she communicates verbally with peers by 25%.
6. She will decrease by 25% the frequency with which she communicates affection by hugging and kissing.

Written Expression

Goal: A will be able to write an original three sentence paragraph, composed of 3-4 word sentences with 70% accuracy.

Objectives:
1. She will write simple sentences correctly from dictation 65% of the time.
2. She will write a simple sentence of her own composition with 60% accuracy.
3. She will master a weekly 10 word spelling list with 80% accuracy.
4. She will use correctly spelled spelling words in simple sentences 60% of the time.

Language Arts

Goal: In a small group she will express herself spontaneously 65% of the time.

Objectives:
1. She will begin to use helping verbs.
2. She will begin to use articles.
3. She will begin to use adjectives.
4. She will use the correct pronoun 60% of the time.

Social Studies and Science

Goal: A will demonstrate comprehension of mid-first grade social studies and science concepts.

Objectives:
1. She will demonstrate understanding of basic vocabulary appropriate to science and social studies with 80% accuracy.
2. She will demonstrate by drawings, pictures, and simple explanaitons her comprehension of the functions of community helpers.

3. She will demonstrate understanding of safety rules by acting out a simulated experience without visual cues 70% of the time.
4. She will demonstrate understanding of basic environmental concepts by making contributions to class experience charts 675% of the time.

Study Skills

Goal: A will demonstrate independent and self-sustained work habits.

Objectives:
1. She will work independently for a 15 minute interval without teacher assistance 70% of the time.
2. She will maintain focus on a speaker for 15 minute intervals without teacher prompt 65% of the time.
3. She will appropriately contribute to a class discussion 3 out of 5 times with 70% accuracy.
4. She will produce self-initiated work without reference to a class mate's work 65% of the time.

EMOTIONAL DISTURBANCE

This is a condition exhibiting one or more of the following characteristics over a long period of time and to a marked degree that adversely affects a child's educational performance:

*An inability to learn that cannot be explained by intellectual, sensory, or health factors

*An inability to build or maintain satisfactory interpersonal relationships with peers and teachers

*Inappropriate types of behavior or feelings under normal circumstances

*A general mood of unhappiness or depression

*A tendency to develop physical symptoms or fears associated with personal or school problems

*Schizophrenia

IEP 1

(Note: It is much more difficult to understand the student's needs when presented in narrative form. Chunking and stripping away unnecessary words is the most effective presentation.)

S.B., Girl, Age 16

Classification: Emotionally Disturbed
Severe psychiatric problems
Mild learning disabilities
Gifted artist, musician

PRESENT LEVELS OF EDUCATIONAL PERFORMANCE

Adaptive functioning

S begins the school day appearing anxious and hyperactive. This usually levels off by third period. She uses minimal speech in class and is largely withdrawn from her peer group. Continued support in this area by all of her instructors is imperative, particularly at the end of class periods when she feels awkward before the bell rings. She is intensively interested in rock music, studying its history, performers and music over the last decade, becoming an expert in this genre. Her interest is so focused and intense that it largely excludes other interests that her peers share. She will retreat into thinking about this music or a related area when she becomes upset or overloaded. Many of the groups and lyrics to songs deal with morose and morbid ideas which she often selects to reflect her feelings when upset or anxious. She has formed a close attachment to her case manager and is permitted to visit him when stressed. Her sensitivity and empathy can cause intense emotional upset depending on the circumstance. She can demonstrate emotional fragility when overwhelmed with school work, shown when she feels unable to complete assignments on time or at the levels expected. She also separates herself from her peers during the school day except for lunch. She is overly sensitive to the problems of other students, sometimes taking on their problems as her own. She will hold in her frustration and fears until they overwhelm her periodically. She received individual counseling sessions either during lunch or the Period 9 Transition class. These are needed for her development of social skills and friendships as well as transition skills. Therefore, neither period is to be used for counseling in the upcoming school year, another time to be scheduled. She also sees a private therapist and is under the care of a treating psychiatrist.

Academics

S is an intelligent and creative student with above average potential except in her areas of disability, which are in math calculation and math reasoning. Problems that impact upon her performance in school and cut across all content areas are homework completion and classroom participation in discussions and related activities. Her areas of strength are in Spanish and Fibers. She is observed to work well with other students but often perceived her participation to be poor to mediocre. She is a hard worked, but needs to use more effort to

61

complete class assignments. Areas of weakness are in test taking, math reasoning and retention, with some difficulty in writing and auditory processing. She easily loses focus, has consistent problems with organization of both time and materials, and does not verbally participate in class, usually saying she does not know. She sits in the front row of each class, gets extra time for tests and quizzes when possible, and has an in-class support teacher.

Transition

S is extremely talented in singing, playing guitar, and writing song lyrics. It is expected that she will attend a music or art school of some kind for post-secondary education. She currently studies music and music theory privately. In addition, she is an equally talented visual artist, with significant drawing and design skills. This interest extends to fashion and jewelry design. In order to facilitate her artistic and creative skills, S needs to learn to seek out activities of interest in her community and initiate involvement with them. At present, she waits for others to create the opportunity for her participation in an activity. She is a member of the Girl Scouts, but needs peers who share her interests in music and in art. It is likely that she will attend and complete a four year college program. While she functions as an independent teenager, her self-regulation needs a great deal of support and attention so that she decreases her moodiness. It is important for her to take ownership of her actions in order to improve responsibility for success both in and out of school. She is to be encouraged to participate in her high school musicals and art exhibits, staff being mindful that she may say she does not want to do an activity because she is fearful of not doing it perfectly. She may display significant rigidity with new ideas, or with a music or art form she thinks she will not enjoy. Nonetheless, the broadening of exposure to a variety of art forms and genres is an important part of her individualized transition program.

The Transition Practicum for her tenth grade year is to provide her with instruction in organizational skills and homework completion. She is to be weaned from the amount of time spent with her case manager in the special education office and develop coping skills to get her through difficult times without the need to leave the classroom. The transition teacher is to sit with her each day and review what needs to be done that night, as well as long term assignments, materials needed, and getting those materials and work into her book bag for classes the next day. All of her teachers need to receive in-service training so that her social and emotional needs can be met during each instructional period, building organizational and building independence. To the degree possible, assistive technology should be explored for her to record her homework, as well as long and short term assignments. Work on test taking strategies and how to handle stress and anxiety must also be a part of her program. S has a history of tutoring in order to catch up on skills and projects missed. Part of her transition programming must teach her to keep up with school assignments before running into trouble because everything is due at the same time. Teachers need to stagger their assignments in such a way that she is not overloaded and can independently manage her time to complete assignments. Considerations are also needed for her lag in auditory processing, organizational difficulties, and how easily she overloads and shuts down.

EDUCATIONAL GOALS AND OBJECTIVES

(Note: There is no measurement in the goal statement because it was not in the evaluation data. Rather, it appears in the objectives based on teacher and parent input.)

Social/Emotional

Goal: S shall demonstrate improved social and emotional functioning.

Objectives:

1. She shall appropriately initiate social interactions with a variety of school peers 80% of the time.
2. She shall demonstrate the ability to participate in a social exchange in topics not of interest to her 70% of the time.
3. She shall demonstrate decreased anxiety at the end of a class period.
4. She shall demonstrate the ability to separate her problems and life experiences from those of her peers 80% of the time.
5. She shall demonstrate increased awareness of her strengths and talents by participating in school activities with peers 70% of the time.
6. She will demonstrate the ability to apply coping strategies during periods of instruction, not leaving the classroom to recover from upset 70% of the time.
7. S will participate in a school sponsored musical activity.
8. S shall participate in extra-curricular activities in areas of her talents and interests.

Expressive language

Goal: S shall improve her expressive language in the classroom.

Objectives:

1. She will answer a question when called upon 90% of the time.
2. She will participate in classroom discussions 70% of the time.
3. She will request a brief break when she is overloaded, but remain nearby the classroom.

Organizational skills

Goal: S shall demonstrate improved independent organizational and study skills.

Objectives:

1. She shall use a calendar which she carries to/from school to record due dates of long and short term assignments 90% of the time.
2. She will establish and adhere to a nightly after-school schedule for completion of her homework 90% of the time. (This homework is not to exceed 90 minutes.)
3. She shall demonstrate the ability to do a task analysis of the sequence needed, from start to finish, for completion of both classwork and homework. This includes:
    A. Organizing her book bag and materials to prepare and complete her homework.
    B. Keep content-related materials organized together in her binder.
    C. Determine the easiest and more difficult assignments, completing the easiest ones first, then going on to the more difficult 60% of the time.
    D. She shall place her completed homework in her binder upon completion, put it in her book bag, and hand it in at school at the appropriate time.
    E. She shall use the 9th period of her school day to complete/clarify homework/classwork for the next day, as well as long term assignments.
    F. S shall inform her 9th period teacher of future tests and assignments 90% of the time, said teacher to already have this information to prompt S if she forgets.

Math calculation and reasoning
(Note: This area should have been divided into two separate categories if sufficient data had been available.)

Goal: S shall demonstrate improved math calculation and reasoning.

Objectives:

1. She will verbalize the steps and sequence needed to solve a math problem of the four basic processes with 80% accuracy.
2. She shall write the solutions to solve basic math problems with 80% accuracy.
3. She shall demonstrate the ability to round off whole numbers with 90% accuracy.
4. She shall demonstrate the ability to calculate liquid, solid, and linear measurements with 60% accuracy.
5. She shall demonstrate mastery of double digit fractions in addition, subtraction and multiplication.
6. She shall check her completed answers with a calculator 100% of the time.
7. She shall demonstrate ability to solve basic math problems in real life 60% of the time

IEP 2

J.B., Boy, Age 14

Classification: Emotionally Disturbed
Primary emotional disturbance
Secondary learning disabilities

PRESENT LEVELS OF EDUCATIONAL PERFORMANCE

Academics

J's educational levels are scattered over a seven year range, indicating the severity of his learning disabilities. His perceptual speed is the GE (grade equivalent) of 10.6, while his auditory memory is severely deficient at a GE of 3.2. Reading is a GE of 8.8, while math, general knowledge and skills are within the 7th grade range. Written language is a GE of 5.5, with severe visual-motor integration functioning at the age equivalent of 8.7. His math skills appear to depend on his environment and the instructional circumstances. He has very poor silent reading comprehension and sentence sequencing ability.

Cognitive Ability

J has achieved an average to above average IQ over successive administrations, each time showing significant subtest scatter. His parents and teacher see him as a very bright child with potential far exceeding that presently displayed. He requires an exceptionally long processing time, with particular difficulty in manipulating and combining information.

Adaptive Behavior

J is a social isolate with a desire to learn and ability to learn if the instruction is presented in short chunks. He is perfectionistic and sensitive concerning his intelligence, reacting negatively to placement with a peer group of less cognitive and academic ability than his own. He is fragile, guarded, and vulnerable, whose macho bravura is used to protect his vulnerability. His concrete view of situations coincides with his underestimation of his own problems. He has ADHD with accompanying mood swings, and with difficulty reacting to failure realistically. He is very attached to his guitar and is motivated by thoughts of a musical career.

Personal/Social Development

J can be a charming, sensitive and attentive teen-ager in a 1-1 setting. He has long-standing anger and distrust toward the school district for what he believes to be their failure to educate him properly. He has suicidal ideations, causing two previous psychiatric admissions to hospitals. He has no close friends. His social skills are considered to be poor, with an inability to handle input from a social situation. He makes minimal eye contact, has an obsession with neatness, and has admitted to occasional substance abuse. He is particularly defensive and cannot tolerate criticism. He responds well to praise and can be extremely persistent. Though he presently feels angry and demoralized, he is challenged by difficult academic tasks.

<u>Language Proficiency</u>

J's verbal functioning is varied, with strengths in the more concrete areas, such as verbal comprehension. His weaknesses are in such areas as verbal relationships. His expressive language is below average, though his teacher indicates he has skills at expressing his ideas. He has moderate deficits in written expressive language, though he does enjoy creating song lyrics.

<u>Physical and Health Status</u>

J has been on Ritalin, but is not always medically compliant. When he does not take Ritalin he often has behavioral difficulties in school with both peers and teaching staff.

EDUCATIONAL GOALS AND OBJECTIVES

<u>Social Skills</u>

Goal: J shall develop age appropriate social skills in the classroom.

Objectives:
1. He shall demonstrate the ability to sit throughout a class period with cuing 4 out of 5 times.
2. He shall demonstrate the ability to sit throughout a class period without cuing 3 out of 5 times.
3. He shall respond appropriately 4 out of 5 times, both verbally and physically, when teachers ask him to do.
4. He will show understanding of established classroom rules by verbally explaining them to the instructor in his own words with 100% accuracy.
5. He will show the ability to follow established classroom rules with cuing 80% of the time.
6. He shall demonstrate the ability to follow the established classroom rules without cuing 70% of the time.

Goal: J shall demonstrate appropriate social interaction skills.

Objectives:
1. He shall demonstrate eye contact when speaking or spoken to 100% of the time.
2. He shall seek out appropriate others to interact with, initiating a "small talk" conversation on a daily basis (weather, holidays, etc.).
3. He will demonstrate appropriate listening skills when being spoken to 8 out of 10 times.
4. He will appropriately respond/answer when spoken to 70% of the time.
5. He will demonstrate the ability to converse on various topics with increasing lengths of time.
6. He shall demonstrate the ability to ask questions without becoming too personal, too aggressive, etc. 90% of the time.
7. He shall demonstrate the ability to develop and maintain at least one friend for a period of time.
8. He shall show ability to maintain friendships within small groups/moderate sized groups for increasing lengths of time

Goal: J shall demonstrate courtesy skills.

Objectives:
1. He shall use polite words on all appropriate occasions, such as Please, Thank You, Excuse me, etc. 100% of the time.
2. He shall allow others to borrow an appropriate something of his, establishing reasonable rules and limits on its use and return.
3. He shall demonstrate the ability to follow the rules when playing games with others 90% of the time.
4. He shall demonstrate the ability to take the initiative to assist others when they need help 4 out of 5 times.
5. He shall use physical contact with others in an appropriate manner 100% of the time.

Goal: J shall demonstrate making a friend skill.

Objectives:
1. He shall demonstrate less perfectionistic habits in both himself and others.
2. He shall indicate friendly responses by smiling appropriately 100% of the time.
3. He shall demonstrate the ability to compliment others by telling someone when J likes something they do 60% of the time.
4. He shall initiate making friends by: seeking out appropriate others to interact with, initiating conversations, taking turns talking, and asking the person to spend time with him.

Goal: J shall demonstrate coping skills.

Objectives:
1. He shall find acceptable ways to occupy his time when he asks to join an activity and the answer is no.
2. He shall express anger by telling someone he is angry without hurting them, and without using obscene language.
3. He shall demonstrate the ability to look away and not answer when someone teases him.
4. When someone tries to hurt/fight with J, he shall first try and walk away, second seek adult intervention, or defend himself appropriately.
5. When someone asks J to do something he cannot do or does not wish to do, he will say NO politely.
6. When events are not going well, J shall seek options by developing a list of options from which he can choose his intervention.

Academics
Math

Goal: J shall develop compensatory strategies for basic math skills.

Objectives:
1. He shall use a calculator 100 % of the time for all basic math work which he has not mastered.

2. He shall show his functioning use of math in applied situations, such as shopping within a budget, ordering merchandise, percentages and discounts.
3. He shall show the ability to balance a check book.
4. He shall demonstrate the conceptual understanding of fractions, namely they are less than 1.
5. He shall be exposed to introductory algebraic concepts with the understanding that he is not expected to solve them independently.

Written Expressive Language

Goal: J shall improve his written expression.

Objectives:
1. He will use a word processor with a spell check to proof read his work.
2. He shall demonstrate the ability to correctly sequence sentences with 70% accuracy.
3. He shall demonstrate the ability to develop topic sentences, supporting details and concluding sentences in paragraph writing with 70% accuracy.
4. He shall demonstrate the ability to write reports on a variety of topics with correct punctuation, grammar and form 70% of the time.
5. He shall demonstrate the ability to write a short expository report, observing correct syntax and style 70% of the time.
6. He shall become aware of the inner rhythm of written language, developing song lyrics that are grammatically correct 80% of the time.

Self- awareness

Goal: J shall improve his emotional functioning.

Objectives:
1. He shall demonstrate an understanding concerning the severity of his problems.
2. He shall demonstrate the ability to react to failure realistically.
3. He shall show the ability to use a less concrete approach to interpreting events by learning the concepts of symbols, metaphor, simile, and allegory.
4. He shall demonstrate an acceptance of his learning disabilities, and emphasize his strengths and not his weaknesses.
5. He shall articulate and demonstrate behaviors associated with improved self-image and self-esteem.
6. He shall show greater tolerance to frustration.
7. He shall show the ability to accept constructive criticism.
8. He shall accept the concerns of others about his behaviors.

HEARING IMPAIRMENT

This is impairment in hearing, whether permanent or fluctuating, that adversely affects a child's educational performance. It is not included under the definition of deafness.

The tendency to "name" or "label" conditions and to believe that one has thereby explained or understood them is an all too human weakness. We see this practice in many areas- political, economic, social, medical, and educational. For some time now, children with an infinite variety of learning problems have been labeled "perceptually" or "neurologically" impaired, as if these terms explain the condition, or, better still, lead to some appropriate remediation. Further, these labels frequently are based on examinations that fail to isolate perception or to determine whether it refers to vision, audition, or touch, and they rarely test the intactness of the nervous system. Evidence for perceptual or neurological impairment is often inferred from performance on a single, poorly validated test.

(Rudel)

IEP 1

E.D., Boy, Age 10

Classification: Hearing Impaired
Extremely curious
Highly motivated
No usable language system
Total Communication

PRESENT LEVELS OF EDUCATIONAL PERFORMANCE

In all content areas- Reading, Language Arts, Arithmetic, Science, Social Studies, Physical Education, and Art, E. achieved a grade of C or satisfactory. It is unknown what he would have had to do in order to get and A or B. Teacher input states that in Communication/Reading he is able to write neater than he usually does if he would write slower and concentrate more. He is identifies pictures from the first 10 lessons of Basic Vocabulary cards containing pictures of objects in the house, food, clothing, and animals. Teacher input is that he uses a structured sentence pattern and is able to read simple sentences and identify familiar nouns and verbs with teacher assistance. He can write capital and lower case letters independently on lined paper. He can identify Who, What, and action words from a series of pictures and/or familiar printed words. He recognizes familiar vocabulary through sign language including foods, animals, clothing, objects in the home, and action verbs. He can imitate the teacher's speech, constructing noun-verb-noun-verb-noun patterns using total communication.

He is in Math #3, having difficulty memorizing addition number facts. He can identify and independently write numbers 0-50 using sign language.

In Speech "He attempts to approximate F, V, and TH with little carry over seen in connected language." In hearing, he responds to loud volume versus soft volume sounds. He can identify verbs run, jump, and walk, with speech reading cues, to produce target speech sounds (a, u, e) when the teacher acts as role model, and can produce I, a, u, oy, I, and a in syllable drills.

In Science he is said to correctly label the stem, leaves and root of a plant, observed the growth of roots, and the reaction of a magnet when placed on a variety of objects. With teacher assistance and using familiar vocabulary, he is able to categorize and compare heavier and lighter objects and can select one or two characteristics of the seasons and seasonal clothing with teacher assistance. In Health he demonstrates the proper steps of good grooming, prevention of the spreading of germs, and has been exposed to grooming vocabulary such as soap, shampoo. Shower, etc. In Social Studies he is aware of certain rules that people follow and that there are 12 months in a year. He is able to independently write his phone number and list at least one feature for Easter, Valentine's Day and Mother's Day.

70

E's cognition, measured by the Performance Scale of the WISC, illustrates subtest scatter showing strengths in Block Design and Object Assembly. Block Design is a timed subtest requiring E to manipulate one inch cubes to reproduce the model presented by the examiner. It measures visual perception, motor coordination, logic, spatial ability, and is excellent in assessing problem solving skills. Object Assembly is also a timed test where tag board puzzle pieces are put together, and there is measuring, organizational skills and planning. The child must sustain attention and perceive spatial relationships.

Weaknesses were found in Picture Arrangement, a timed subtest that requires the arrangement of pictures into a logical, sequential order to tell a story. It also measures the ability to determine cause and affect relationships. Difficulty on this test shows problems with integrating thoughts and specifying cause and effect relationships. E appears to have trouble in understanding directions, especially of abstract concepts, as well as in visual motor problems involving complex visual stimuli. In Math he was able to add one digit numbers less than 10. In Reading, he is at the readiness level, but not yet ready to complete the primary level.

When interacting with his environment, E is shy, observant and cautious, yet carries a sense of independence about him. In addition, he has an excellent sense of humor. Once at ease, he is more outgoing and animated, enjoying tasks given to him. He is extremely curious, highly motivated, and capable of having a relationship with others despite his absence of words. In his neighborhood, he is sought out by children on the block. He is experiencing increasing frustration due to his inability to comprehend rules of games in small and large group situations. He plays several kinds of board games, participates in many kinds of sports, and is exceptionally good at remembering routes and how things are put together. He has a variety of interests but requires language in order to help him understand the rules of the game, such as baseball.

He has experienced severe problems on the school bus this year. His hearing aids have been pulled out, he has been spit on, and his parents are concerned for his safety and well-being while on the bus.

A new hearing aid evaluation found that he is not receiving adequate benefit from his current hearing aids and another model was recommended. It was stated to be essential that E be enrolled in a training program to assist him in making increased auditory perceptions. He relies on a combination of sign language, idiosyncratic gesture and speech to communicate with familiar people in his environment. Spoken language was obtained by passing the Telex microphone to him as a sign to talk. He strings single words together to tell a picture story. He can imitate two word combinations if words are tapped out for him. When forced to rely on speech reading alone, he has extreme difficulty. He evidences awareness of sound and use of his residual hearing. He is unable to vary his voice pitch from high to low sound, slight variation noted when using a vibrator. The addition of vibro-tactile information consistently raised his perception scores to 100%. Phoneme perception was poor regardless of the form of amplification used. He has no functional language system.

Goal Headings

(Note: These goal headings organized the weaknesses in the Current Status narrative, applying task analysis in some cases.)

*Discrimination between environmental sounds (list sounds/degree of discrimination)
*Mastery of three phonemes (name and describe type of mastery required)
*Develop a functional language system using total communication to include:
*Development of two consistent utterances of noun, verb, adjective relationships
*Identifying all colors
*Matching/naming like items
*Naming/identifying opposites
*Develop concept of rhyming
*Language of number/size
*Mastery of common prepositions
*Vocabulary of shapes
*Vocabulary of body parts
*Language of outdoor games and play equipment
*Language of cooking
*Language of social amenities
*Language of entertainment (TV, movies, computer games, etc.)
*Language of cause/effect
*Receptive/expressive mastery of the 100 most commonly used words (grades 1-3)
*Connect receptive/expressive language to sight word vocabulary
*Connect signing vocabulary and writing skills

EDUCATIONAL GOALS AND OBJECTIVES

Expressive Language

Goal: E shall develop a total communication-based, functional language system.

Objectives:
1. E shall use his glottis, hard and soft palette, and tongue to correctly demonstrate single consonant placement 60% of the time.
2. He shall demonstrate correct long vowel placement 60% of the time.
3. He shall demonstrate short vowel placement 60% of the time.
4. He shall develop age appropriate skill in the four cheremes of sign language: configuration, movement, orientation and place of contact 65% of the time.
5. He shall combine the four cheremes to form sign vocabulary with 70% accuracy.
6. He shall demonstrate the ability to visually discriminate lip. Mouth and tongue placement and shape in speech reading activities 60% of the time.

7. He shall develop his residual hearing by demonstrating discrimination between the environmental sounds of: telephone, airplane, car horn, doorbell, etc. to the maximum extent as measured in his most recent testing.
8. He shall develop and demonstrate perception of duration, intensity and pitch 20% of the time.
9. He shall develop and demonstrate consistency in perception of the supra-segmental features most easily perceived (specify) 90% of the time.

Receptive Language
(Note: The list of objectives is not measured, and is based upon concepts in the regular education curriculum by grade. Measurements must be added.)

Goal: E shall demonstrate receptive language skills to a 4.0 age level with integration of total communication for contextual clues, speech reading, signing, and body language.

Objectives:
1. He shall demonstrate the ability to speech read words for each of the areas of receptive language listed below with 65% accuracy.
2. He shall demonstrate a mastery of the understanding/labeling of all primary colors.
3. He shall demonstrate understanding of the concepts of:
Matching
Opposite
Size
Shape
Amount (more/less)
Addition (combine/put together)
Subtraction (take away/less)
Direction words (Behind, in front of, over, under, below, forward, backward)
Body part names
Personal needs vocabulary: hunger, thirst, hurt, sick, afraid, hot, cold, love, dislike, etc.
Names of clothing, toys, games, TV programs, play equipment, playground equipment
Room names in school and at home
Language of social amenities: please, thank you, you're welcome, excuse me, I'm sorry.
Because (cause/effect)
Names of commonly used buildings/places
Animal names, domestic/zoo
Food names
Eating utensil names
Health/hygiene vocabulary: doctor, nurse, bandage, thermometer, toothbrush, etc.
Seasonal vocabulary
Transportation mode names: car, place, train, bus, etc.
Kitchen utensil names
Job names: policeman, fireman, etc.
Action names: dig, blow, build, break, sit, stand, etc.

Regional vocabulary: cowboy, Indian
Circus vocabulary
Musical instrument vocabulary
Bedtime vocabulary
Calendar vocabulary
Nature/environment vocabulary
Clock/time vocabulary
Money vocabulary
School vocabulary: black board, principal, teacher

Expressive language

Goal: E shall demonstrate expressive language skills using total communication to a 3.0 language age level.

Objectives:
1. Through utilization of total communication, he shall spontaneously express a minimum of five words per category in the areas listed under Receptive Language with 65% accuracy.
2. He shall spontaneously express noun/verb, adjective/noun relationships 50% of the time.
3. He shall develop intelligible, spontaneous oral language for classroom, social, home and community use by 25% from baseline measurements.
4. He shall demonstrate the ability to write independently selected vocabulary words and phrases from each of the categories under Receptive Language with 70% accuracy.
5. He shall develop a sight vocabulary to a 1.5 grade level in reading.
6. He shall decode a specified list of word families with 65% accuracy.
7. He shall demonstrate spelling skills to a 1.5 grade level.
8. He shall demonstrate math skills to a 1.5 grade level with 65% accuracy.

Social/Emotional

Goal: E shall improve his social and emotional functioning.

Objectives:
1. He will display less frustration in understanding multistep directions given orally 2 out of 5 times.
2. He will spontaneously initiate a social contact with a peer on an on-going basis at an appropriate time with 50% accuracy.
3. He will demonstrate the ability to engage in social conversation/exchange with a peer/teacher 60% of the time.
4. He will display less stubbornness when requested to complete or do an activity.

5. He will ask for help in the classroom 60% of the time, rather than sit silently, not understanding what is to be done.
6. He will display increased motivation and incentive to learn and apply total communication in classroom and social situations.
7. He will function independently in specified situations 3 out of 5 times.
8. He will display increased social skills in a 1-1, small group and large group settings with increases from baseline measurements in these settings.

Study Skills

Goal: E will demonstrate improvement in study skills.

Objectives:

1. He will demonstrate the ability to understand his assignment before leaving the classroom.
2. He will display the ability to find/use an appropriate room at home/school to do his homework.
3. He will demonstrate the ability to organize his materials.
4. He will demonstrate the ability to sequence the order of the completion of his homework- what to do first, second, third, etc. with 70% accuracy.
5. He will demonstrate the ability to check his work before handing it in with 75% accuracy.
6. He will place the work in a location at home so as to have it ready to take to school the next day 4 out of 5 times.
7. He will remember to hand in his homework 80% of the time.
8. He will remember to bring all school communications home and give them to his parents 75% of the time.

Related Services

Speech therapy, 1-1, 5 times per week, 60 minute sessions
Staff training in total communication with monthly consultations following intensive in-service
Parent training in total communication
Extended school year
Pre and post testing by licensed teachers of the hearing impaired

Evaluative criteria

(Note: Evaluation can be in a separate section if deemed appropriate.)

Parent will be co-evaluator of program implementation
Evaluation at 3 months, 6 months and 9 months into the program by licensed evaluators of the hearing impaired.

MENTAL RETARDATION/INTELLECTUAL DISABILITY

This is a category reflecting significantly sub-average, general intellectual functioning, existing concurrently with deficits in adaptive behavior, and manifested during the developmental period that adversely affects a child's educational performance. Though the term still exists in IDEA, it was changed in 2007 to Intellectual and Developmental Disabilities by experts and organizations in the field. At the federal level, Rosa's Law, P.L. 111-256, replaced "mental retardation" with "intellectual disability". This was a precursor to the publication of DSM V in 2013 by the American Psychiatric Association who renamed mental retardation "intellectual disability/intellectual developmental disorder". It defined intelligence as "a general mental ability that involves reasoning, problem solving, planning, abstract thought, comprehension of complex ideas, judgment, academic learning and learning from experience. It remains divided into four categories: mild, moderate, severe and profound. The new emphasis focuses on academic learning, social understanding, practical understanding, and issues of gullibility and credulity.

IEP 1

S.D., Boy, Age 17

Mild retardation
Williams Syndrome

PRESENT LEVELS OF EDUCATIONAL PERFORMANCE

NOTE: The present levels of functioning below were taken from sworn testimony during a due process hearing. There were major disputes over S.D.'s levels of functioning between the parents and the school district. This IEP was written at the Hearing Officer's request, based upon the fact statements of witnesses.

S is a shy, laid back, and extremely gullible teenager, who is significantly smaller in size than his peer group. He is not able to read body language and has poor judgment skills. He does not know how to use leisure time and needs time to regroup and relax after a school day. Cognitively he functions higher than a moderately impaired student, and has a wider spread of abilities than the mildly retarded population with whom he is now placed. He has weak auditory processing, does not generalize information, and would benefit from a learning disabled orientation to his programming.

Academically, he decodes at a third to fourth grade level, with comprehension at the First grade level. He can add and subtract pennies and nickels separately but is unable to mix pennies, nickels and dimes and count the amount of change. He has never been exposed to liquid or solid measurement, and his reading rate has gone down by two grade levels. He has a large void in his general fund of information and needs organizational skills in all areas. He has difficulty with ball skills and has weak eye-hand coordination. No vocational skills have been introduced or explored.

He has weak survival skills relative to his independence. He does not know how to use public transportation or make decisions relating to buying. He has problems with reading labels and comprehending the contents of his purchase. He has some difficulties with toileting, requiring more advance notice to avoid soiling himself.

S.D. has severe language needs. At present his answers are irrelevant in the classroom, and he cannot give specific answers to classroom questions. He is perceived not to understand what the teacher says during instruction, comprehending only 37% of the classroom work. He does not speak spontaneously in a group setting and needs reinstruction every week, forgetting much of what he had learned. He has great difficulty with generalization and needs intensive daily language therapy. His needs include learning language structures and concepts (naming, doing, describing) and pragmatics and generalization of social language skills. In addition, he has weak word finding skills.

EDUCATIONAL GOALS AND OBJECTIVES

Reading

Goal: S shall demonstrate improvement in reading related objectives to a mid-second grade level at least 65% of the time.

Objectives:
1. He shall demonstrate an understanding of the use of punctuation, exclamation points, commas, and question marks to assist in comprehension of paragraphs/stories at his grade level.
2. He shall identify details in a paragraph and short story.
3. He shall identify the main idea and subordinate ideas in a paragraph.
4. He shall develop increased understanding of abstract vocabulary.
5. He shall provide an appropriate antonym, synonym, and homonym from a given stimuls word.
6. He shall recognizer cause and effect when reading a story, answering "why".
7. He shall retell a story in the correct sequence of events.
8. He shall follow written directions, gradually increasing the number to 3 with 80% accuracy.

Written Expressive Language

Goal: S shall demonstrate improved written expressive language to a mid-second to third grade level a minimum of 60% of the time.

Objectives:
1. S shall improve sentences by using more descriptive language such as adjectives.
2. He shall write the correct synonym, antonym, and homonym from basic vocabulary items such as tall/short, big/small, etc.
3. He shall write a complex sentence using at least one conjunction.
4. He shall write a short friendly letter.
5. He shall write a paragraph with an introduction, body and conclusion, using three sentences to be increased as his ability develops.

Money

Goal: S shall improve his money management skills to a functional level 55% of the time.

Objectives:
1. He shall be able to add and subtract pennies, nickels and dimes.
2. He shall demonstrate the understanding of the amount of a quarter by counting 25 pennies.
3. He shall make change for a dime.
4. He shall make change for a quarter.
5. He shall make change of a dollar.

6. He shall make change for $5 using one dollar bills.
7. He shall demonstrate improvement of understanding of money concepts relating to:
   A. Receiving a salary
   B. Household expenses
   C. Savings and budgeting
8. He shall demonstrate improved understanding of money management by:
   A. Use of a coin vending machine
   B. Money on a class trip
   C. Planning a class party
   D. Purchasing food items/clothing.

Computer skills

Goal: S shall demonstrate initial competency in the use of computers following an evaluation of his knowledge/ability.

Objectives:
1. He shall increase his ability to follow 3 step directions with 65% accuracy.
2. He shall learn the rudiments of word processing software.
3. He shall improve his keyboarding skills to ___words per minute.
4. He shall increase verbal and the ability to classify skills.

Life Skills

Goal: S shall improve his life skills to demonstrate self-sufficiency and independence with 65% accuracy/completion of objectives.

Objectives:
1. S shall follow through on specific chores/responsibilities in school/home with cuing, fading the cues as skills develop.
2. He shall learn conversational skills relating to the telephone using role playing.
3. He shall understand concepts relating to sex education: dating, reproduction, masturbation, drugs.
4. He shall refrain from inappropriate sexual activity in school or on the school bus.

Speech/Language

(Note: There is no ability to measure these goals and objectives. The line for measurement is there for school personnel to complete.)

Goal: S shall demonstrate improved expressive language skills to a ___age level with ___% consistency (TBD by speech/language therapist).

Objectives:
1. He shall improve his ability to generalize rule-governed noun plurals into speech.
2. He shall improve his use of regular plural words.

3. He shall improve his use of irregular plural words.
4. He shall improve his ability to form sentences using possessive nouns.
5. He shall improve his use of first, second, and third person pronouns.
6. He shall improve his use of correct verb forms and tenses.
7. He shall improve his ability to appropriately add ING to words.
8. He shall improve use of the present tense while talking about events in the past.
9. He shall improve his use of past tense when speaking about the past.
10. He shall decrease over use and generalization of the past tense.
11. He shall improve use of both regular and irregular past tense (to be/to go, etc.)
12. He shall increase in ability to correctly select prepositions.
13. He shall decrease omission of prepositions when appropriate.
14. He shall improve his ability to use word definitions.
15. He shall increase use of new vocabulary words.
16. He shall improve his ability to produce multi-syllable words during spontaneous speech.
17. He shall begin to use descriptive language.
18. He shall use antonym, synonym and homonym in appropriate contexts when asked.
19. He shall use multiple meaning words in the appropriate context.

Vocational

Goal: S shall demonstrate pre-vocational skills.

Objectives:
1. He shall explore job related areas emphasizing his strengths and individual interests.
2. He shall role-ply interviews, positive work attitudes and potential problems relating to a work setting.
3. He shall inhibit exhibiting inappropriate emotions at work or school.
4. He shall refrain from inappropriate sexual activity in school or on the school bus.

Reading comprehension

Goal: S shall demonstrate improved reading comprehension skills through use of school-related content areas.

Objectives:
1. He shall identify the main and subordinate idea(s) in a story.
2. He shall recognize and identify cause and effect when listening to a story.
3. He shall improve his ability to predict outcomes when listening to a story.
4. He shall demonstrate improved understanding of temporal relationships.
5. He shall improve his ability to understand spatial and directional relationships.
6. He shall improve his ability to use figurative language and idioms.

Sequencing

Goal: S shall demonstrate improved sequencing ability to 5 steps with 75% accuracy.

Objectives:
1. He shall locate details in a sentence/short story.
2. He shall be able to retell a story in proper sequence.
3. He shall improve his ability to organize the sequences of events in his spoken communication.
4. He shall improve his use of personal experiences to demonstrate understanding of sequence and closure.

Sentence Structure

Goal: S shall demonstrate improved sentence structure.
Objectives:
1. He shall be able to use negative sentences.
2. He shall produce simple declarative sentences, gradually expanding complexity (compound, use of direct object, etc.).
3. He shall improve comprehension of sentences with general negations.

Pragmatics of language

Goal: S shall demonstrate measureable improvement in his social, emotional, and interpersonal life through improved use of pragmatic language.
Objectives:
1. S shall increase his awareness of appropriate behaviors with strangers.
2. He shall increase his socialization skills with peers.
3. He shall initiate conversations with peers in an appropriate manner.
4. He shall maintain eye contact when meeting new people and when ending a conversation.
5. He shall give accurate responses to questions.
6. He shall curtail irrelevant verbalizations.
7. He shall reduce excessive verbalizations.
8. He shall reply to a speaker's statements without changing the topic to irrelevant/tangential subjects.
9. He shall use increased verbalization of feelings during stressful and normal activities.
10. He shall who or to what he is referring in a conversation.
11. He shall reduce his distractibility to background stimuli.
12. He shall improve his ability to explain to the listener what or to whom he is referring in conversation.
13. He shall improve his ability to focus on the needs of his conversation partner.
14. He shall improve his ability to ask questions.

IEP 2

J.G., Girl, Age 16

Classification: Mentally Retarded
Excellent social skills
Severe academic weaknesses
Poor self-esteem
Mild-moderate retardation

PRESENT LEVELS OF EDUCATIONAL PERFORMANCE

(Note: There are no numbers in the current status, so that subsequent testing is needed. Task analysis is used in developing the objectives.)

J's adaptive functioning shows high motivation to do what is asked of her and remarkable astuteness in people skills. She has a charming personality, is a diligent worker, and has good awareness of social rules and conventions. She responds to visual demonstration, shows perseverance and is generally attentive. She has a lively and appealing manner, as well as a strong and resilient personality. Weaknesses included frequent headaches, being too literal and concrete, language problems, visual perception problems, attentional weaknesses, conceptualization, abstract reasoning, and a poor information base. She is seen to sacrifice her own interests for social acceptance. She expresses great unhappiness in her present program and placement and is continuously unhappy and discontent when she talks about school with her parents.

Her cognitive scores placed her in the mentally deficient range, with a 27 point difference between verbal and performance IQ. She has difficulty with synthesizing elements, giving up before the allotted time, and visual motor processing. She always feels nervous and has problems in reproducing geometric figures. Academically she has severe deficits in all areas, with an inability to understand, integrate and use spoken language. She has an inability to follow oral directions, and forming verbal ideas into a logical sequence. She has problems with visual and short term memory, is easily distracted, and has major deficits in word identification. However, her decoding skills surpass her comprehension skills. She is unable to evaluate what is read and to grasp those ideas. Test taking is difficult for her, and she is unable to write any form of report. She is mocked by her classmates when she does not understand the classwork or discussion.

GOALS AND OBJECTIVES

Expressive Language

Goal: J shall demonstrate the ability to rephrase what she has read.

Objectives:
1. She shall express in her own language the essential information read with 75% accuracy.

82

2. She shall distinguish between essential and nonessential material presented.
3. She shall verbally identify the main idea and supporting ideas from written information with 75% accuracy.
4. She shall verbally identify cause and effect in both read and observed events with 75% accuracy.
5. She shall verbally compare and contrast both read and observed events and information with 75% accuracy.
6. She shall verbally demonstrate the ability to summarize a story with 80% accuracy.
7. She shall demonstrate increased use of new vocabulary in her rephrasing as measured by ____.

Written Language

Goal: J shall demonstrate improved written expressive language.

Objectives:
1. She shall demonstrate the ability to proof-read her written work to a mid-4th grade level with 70% accuracy.
2. She shall use visual imagery in completing writing assignments 60% of the time.
3. She shall take notes from written assignments with 70% accuracy.
4. She shall apply Who, What, When, Where, Why and How to all of her writing assignments with 90% accuracy.

Receptive Language

Goal: J shall demonstrate improved auditory processing/receptive language.

Objectives:
1. She shall follow 3 step oral directions with 65% accuracy in group settings and 80% accuracy in 1-1 settings.
2. She shall demonstrate perceptions of beginning, ending and rhyming sounds with 65% accuracy.
3. She shall develop the ability to select a specific sound from background sounds with 90% accuracy.
4. She shall develop the ability to identify and label adjectives with 90% accuracy.
5. She shall identify and label verbs with 90% accuracy.
6. She shall demonstrate understanding of units of thought pertaining to Who, What, When, Where, Why and How questions with 75% accuracy.
7. She shall demonstrate the ability to categorize words into categories (occupations, states, types of clothing, etc.) with 75% accuracy.

Goal: J shall demonstrate improved auditory association.

Objectives:
1. She will develop the ability to determine same, different and opposite relationships presented receptively 70% of the time.

2. She shall show an understanding of cause and effect with 80% accuracy.
3. She shall predict the outcome or anticipate what will happen next in an auditory situation with 75% accuracy.
4. She shall demonstrate the ability to identify incongruities in a situation with 80% accuracy.
5. She will comprehend vocabulary of time relationships with 70% accuracy.
6. She shall show comprehension of vocabulary of space relationships with 80% accuracy.
7. She will derive and complete verbal analogies with 60% accuracy.
8. She shall provide alternate solutions in problem solving with 70% accuracy.
9. She shall understand multiple meanings of words with 60% accuracy.
10. She shall demonstrate the ability to determine fact from fiction with 70% accuracy.
11. She shall be able to draw inferences from both what she hears and reads with 50% accuracy.
12. She shall understand figures of speech (It's raining cats and dogs.) with 80% accuracy.
13. She will demonstrate the ability to distinguish between relevant and irrelevant ideas to the topic with 70% accuracy.

Goal: J shall improve her auditory memory.

Objectives:
1. She shall demonstrate recall of meaningful patterns of 3-4 words through 9-10 words with 70%-100% respectively.
2. She shall develop recall of the sequenced patterns of numbers with 60% accuracy.
3. She shall recall information and relay it to her teacher and parent at the end of the school day, two days, and three days later with 100%-70% accuracy respectively.
4. She shall develop recall of rote memory material with 80% accuracy.
5. She shall recall verbal instructions in the correct sequence with 80% accuracy.
6. She shall be able to discriminate small differences and likenesses in auditorily presented pairs with 70% accuracy.

Self- image and self esteem

Goal: J shall improve her self-image and self-esteem.

Objectives:
1. She will not sacrifice her own interests for social acceptance by peers as measured by _____.
2. She will show acceptance of her learning disability as demonstrated by ____.
3. She will not apologize for giving wrong answers.
4. She will not "put herself down" in order to evoke sympathy.

Goal: J shall become an independent learner.

Objectives:
1. She shall learn to use the bold print headings in texts for study, organizing and review purposes with 90% accuracy.

2. She shall independently diagram/identify the grammar of sentences to aide her in understanding the information with 90% accuracy.
3. She will develop the strategies of visualization, rephrasing and note taking with 80% accuracy.
4. She shall complete home work, and short and long term assignments with 90%, 80% and 70% accuracy respectively.
5. She will read material once to gain the general idea with 90% accuracy.
6. She will read the same material twice to gain more details with 80% accuracy.
7. She will identify the WWWWWH (who, what, when, where, why, how) questions concerning her reading with 80% accuracy.
8. She will be able to summarize with confidence the study information learned as a result of implementing these objectives with 75% accuracy.

Math

Goal: J shall demonstrate application of math computation to life-skills activities.

Objectives:
1. She will show her ability to tell time to the minute with 90% accuracy.
2. She shall master making change of any coin or dollar combination up to $20.00 with 70% accuracy.
3. She shall master use of liquid measurements (cup, pint, quart, gallon).
4. She shall be able to convert liquid measurements at #3 with 70% accuracy.
5. She shall demonstrate mastery of solid measurement (ounces, pounds).
6. She shall convert solid measurements from one to the other with 70% accuracy.
7. She shall master linear measurement (inches, feet, yards, mile).
8. She will convert linear measurements with 70% accuracy.

Fund of Information

Goal: J shall demonstrate increased fund of general information.
Objectives:
1. She will read one selected newspaper story daily, summarizing its content with 70% accuracy.
2. She will listen to one televised news program daily and summarize what she heard with 65% accuracy.
3. She will be able to connect the events at #1-2 above and discuss their content with 70% accuracy.
4. She will show the ability to use new vocabulary words from #1-2 above within self-constructed sentences with 65% accuracy.
5. She will demonstrate basic knowledge of events in American History with 70% accuracy.
6. She will demonstrate basic science concepts with 60% accuracy.

MULTIPLE DISABILITIES

This means concomitant impairments (such as mental retardation/blindness or mental retardation /orthopedic impairment), the combination of which causes such severe educational needs that they cannot be accommodated in special education programs solely for one of the impairments. This does not include deaf-blindness.

I call for an education that inculcates in students an understanding of major disciplinary ways of thinking. The disciplines that I have singled out are science, mathematics, the arts, and history. Within those disciplinary families, it is not important which disciplines or topics are featured...instead, students should probe with sufficient depth a manageable set of examples so that they come to see how one thinks and acts in the manner of a scientist, a geometer, an artist, an historian.

(Gardner)

IEP 1

(Note: The term "Twice Exceptional" refers to students who are gifted in one or more areas and also classified. Both the gift and the disability must be addressed so as to meet adaptive behavior need. Giftedness alone cannot be factored into special education eligibility.)

N. K., Boy, Age 12

Classification: Multiply Disabled
ADHD, Dysgraphia, Emotional disturbance
Twice Exceptional

PRESENT LEVELS OF EDUCATIONAL PERFORMANCE

The most important factor in developing a program for N is to understand the nature and needs of being Twice Exceptional. Stress occurs when there is insufficient opportunity to connect with his gifts, behavior is misinterpreted, and there is decreased involvement in enrichment experiences. Stress is relieved by letting him follow his strengths/interests, using new learning to achieve personally valued goals. His world view is impervious to outside standards and can lead to suicide gestures. He rejects his "rehabilitative duty…and tries to protect himself against self-doubt, self-hatred, or even suicide by refusing to buy into the school's reward system "(Nowak, 2001). Research is consistent regarding descriptors and essential program elements (Trail, 2011) that must be in his program. Research citations are provided for teaching staff so that they understand that N's mixture of giftedness and disability provides them with a challenge to meet his unique needs and the importance of understanding his fragility and state of mind as a result of being twice exceptional. These include:

Hatred of drill/practice
Poor handwriting
Easily distracted
Perfectionistic
Divergent thinker
Curiosity/constant questioning
Lack of organizational skills
Difficulty completing assignments in a timely manner
Sophisticated sense of humor
Difficulty with linear thinking
Keeping the challenge to their giftedness through advanced material
Support of social/emotional needs

Dysgraphia is a common in N's population and in N's case because the hand cannot move as quickly as the mind. There is no cure for dysgraphia, a neuro-motor impairment, so that technology must be utilized throughout instructional time. Software is needed to address math/science equations, scanning worksheets, etc. A workstation in the classroom with a printer and scanner will also be needed.

CATEGORIES OF INSTRUCTION

Written expressive language   Computer software use

Written expressive language	Computer software use
Spelling	Not able to use cursive writing
Grammar mechanics	Use of note taking software
Run-on sentences	Speech to text dictation
Expanded writing output	AT to assist in organizational skills
Adding details to product	

Social/Emotional	-------	Self-regulation
Aggression		Going to bed on time
Quick temper		Getting to school on time
Breaks classroom rules		Completing tests
Lies		
Faulty judgment, reasoning, insight		
Sometimes cheats		
Some sense of hopelessness		

Eligibility Category

Multiply Disabled- N has concomitant impairments (dysgraphia, ADHD, emotional disturbance, twice exceptionality) the combination of which causes such severe educational needs that they cannot be accommodated in special education programs solely for one of the impairments.

Related Services:

Mentor, 1-1, 1 hour per week in computer technology or Science

In-service training for professional staff in the nature/needs of twice exceptional students and N in particular- 10 hours

Staff training in computer software to be used

Establish personal computer/printer location to integrate into instructional setting

Dragon Naturally Speaking software

Counseling 1X per week, 20 minutes

Psychological Summary

N is a 13.2 year old boy in seventh grade. His school performance declined from prior superior functioning and performance with concerns about completion of homework, classwork, attendance, and behavior. The recent administration of the WISC-IV found superior functioning with FSIQ of 121. His visual perceptual processing was in the Average range, with a 33 point spread between that 61% ile score as compared to his Superior score of 95%ile in VCI. He had weaknesses in Matrix Reasoning with a score of 37%ile and Visual Recall of 14%ile, demonstrating visual processing difficulty in whole to part to whole relationships, visuospatial patterns, and nonverbal concepts. These problems are common to students with dysgraphia and organizational difficulties. The Bender Visual Motor Gestalt Test, 2nd Edition, found a 71 point discrepancy between his highest and lowest performance of visual motor integration skills. On the Copy task he performed at the 85%ile, while on the Recall task he scored at the 14th %ile. This suggests that his short term visual memory skills are below age expectations. This has strong implications for analysis of his Twice Exceptionality and the frustration he experiences in school related tasks that involve organization and written output.

Teacher input gave input about his behavior within the classroom. He was Average in all areas of Math. In the reading/language arts accelerated program he scored in the Clinically Significant range for conduct problems, atypicality, withdrawal, social skills and behavior symptoms. He was At Risk for externalizing problems, aggression, depression, attention, learning, leadership, and functional communication and study skills. Other scores were average. The results, however, must be interpreted with caution because they do not factor in the characteristics, nature and needs of being twice exceptional. All of these clinically significant areas are common when academic, social and emotional needs are not met. This is true of N whose functioning has deteriorated in direct proportion to the written work required, as well as his boredom and frustration with the manner in which his computer access has been handled at school, and the pressure on him at home to complete his school work.

Educational Evaluation

During the 1-1 evaluation, N was very pleasant and cooperative. He focused and understood all directions. Response rate for answering questions was appropriate. He tended to respond impulsively when asked to respond to a writing prompt. He complained that his hand hurt from writing but kept working. He stated that math was his best subject, though his favorite subject was physical education. He enjoys playing basketball and is on the swim team outside of school. Social studies is his least favorite subject, uninterested in the material. He stated that he usually does his homework, but admitted that there were times during school when he did not complete work. He stated that he wanted to get his lowest final grade in social studies since he doesn't like the subject, was disappointed with an 85, and was angry. Test scores ranged from 99%ile in Story Recall to a 70%ile in Broad Written Language, and 63%ile in Writing Samples, or a 36 point discrepancy between highest and lowest performance. His twice exceptionality is confirmed with the discrepancy of these scores and the superior potential he displays.

Social History

Ms. N is a single mother and used a sperm donor to conceive N. He knows about his conception and is aware that he will be given information on how to contact his biological father when he turns 18. The mother reports that N was tardy 17 times and absent 16 times during the school year. This occurred because N refused to wake up, saying he was "exhausted." When his mother asked about school refusal he replied "you aren't listening, it's not that I don't want to go to school, I am tired/exhausted." Mom says that N finds writing difficult and that he is not happy with what he is able to put down on paper. It is not as "creative" or "in-depth" as what he is thinking or what he might say. She reports that his teachers indicate a lack of focus and his grades are impacted by lack of doing homework. He has begun to lie to cover up that he is not doing his work. His in-school benchmarks are high but he does not want to do the actual work.

The mother's relationship with N has greatly declined in the last 18 months. She reports that he is antagonistic, curt, or rude with her. He had a close relationship with his grandfather who passed away in April. N knows about two other families who have children using the same sperm donor and is close with one of the families. She is concerned that he needs more structure, consistency, and follow-through during the school day. She notes that it appears he is standing in his own way for success and that it is really hard for him not having a dad. The mother is also concerned regarding N's attachment to electronics in that he will do anything to access it, regardless of the consequences.

An independent physician diagnosed N with ADHD and ODD. He takes 10 mg time release Adderall daily, 3mg melatonin nightly to help regulate his sleep, sees a psychiatrist for medication oversight, and a counselor once a week. He has also met with a tutor for two months for academic and organizational reasons.

Occupational Therapy Evaluation

N was referred because of the mother's concern about dysgraphia. He exhibits some difficulty with self-regulation regarding arrival at school and for initiation and completion of writing assignments.

Psychiatric Evaluation

N is an exceptionally bright boy with some of the typical by-product eccentricities in ADHD: irregular concentration and some disorganization even though medicated. His exhaustion is related to diminished sleep by way of manipulating TV, electronic devices, video games, etc. As features of his ODD he becomes irritable and snarling toward his mother, using surprisingly bad language. It is especially true now, as his mother is perennially dissatisfied with his academic non-compliance and near disastrous grades, considering his potential and underlying brilliance. He is competitive, worried that someone will beat him in an activity, and has faulty judgment, reasoning and insight. He has an occasional sense of hopelessness and suicidal thoughts that are not extreme. In addition, he has a disorder of written expression and manipulative and narcissistic personality traits.

Central Auditory Processing Evaluation

N has normal hearing skills

Teacher Input

English/Language Arts

His grades of U and D are affected because of accumulating missing homework assignments. He hands in incomplete or completely incorrect work. The lack of personal responsibility for short and long term assignments impacts on his grade. Understanding concepts is easy for him. He reads above grade level with excellent oral fluency and comprehension skills. He makes deeper textual connections than his peers, exhibiting his critical and inferential skills, even with challenging texts. He struggles with written expression. He has creative ideas and the ability to support and elaborate them with details, but needs to put that into his writing. Study guides, notes and graphic organizers have been given to him, in addition to the opportunity to type assignments on the computer and to take assessments online. These have helped him when used. He also has the option of using voice dictation on Microsoft Word for writing assignments so that he does not have to worry about typing them. At times he can lack focus. He related appropriately to teachers and classmates and appears well liked.

Math

He is in a collaborative math class, earning a U in the Advanced Math Track. He did not complete homework and classwork and required much supervision. He was transferred to the lower track in January. He is always respectful and appropriate in the new class and enjoys its small groups for instruction and remediation as needed.

Social Studies

He is in a collaborative class, earning a B- and C-. His grades are affected mostly by the zeros in his homework grade. He also suffers from poor personal management and lack of attentiveness in taking in class assignments and finishing long term projects. He sacrifices speed for accuracy of content. He is very successful in understanding material at face value but refuses to expand his answers. He fails to complete assignments. He can get defiant and refuse to do an assignment, but the majority of the time he is easy to redirect and very personable. He struggles with higher order thinking questions because responses require writing, which he resists. His use of and obsession with the computer unfortunately leads to inefficiency. He works effectively with peers but seems to prefer working alone. He does not enjoy teachers checking up on him or making sure he uses the technology appropriately.

Science

He is enthusiastic in Science and the gifted class, but homework is a problem. He understands concepts and makes excellent connections, but needs to review them in order to retain them. He is generally on task with a good disposition, preferring to do things in his own way and time. He earned an A- and B+.

Parent Input

The mother sees her son's problems through the lens of him being both gifted and disabled. She knows and agrees that he has ADHD, ODD, dysgraphia and an emotional disturbance. She believes that it is imperative to integrate his areas of gift with his deficits, so that through the use of his strengths the deficits can be improved. She has seen him steadily deteriorate since the beginning of the school year because of his lack of success in school and the pressures put upon him to organize and produce written work. Because of N's growing despair concerning his school status and having his computer taken away, he verbalized that he wished he was dead, that a lightning bolt would just come down and kill him. This was said after the school took away his computer for essays and did not tell him when he would get it back. He said it was the same as cutting off his hands. He was being forced to hand in written work and deprived of the only tool that would permit him to meet those requirements. Technology and the appropriate software must be infused throughout his school day into each class and content area. He is now at 4 Winds Hospital, originally taken to Hackensack Hospital. He is in great pain and is extremely fragile. He needs specialized instruction that utilizes appropriate technology in that he will never be able to use handwriting effectively. He needs to learn acceptable outlets for his frustration and anger, to inhibit his striking out, and to take responsibility for his actions, recognizing that he is 13. He needs to learn that life is not always fair. He needs to learn that it is not necessary to always win or always have a perfect product. He needs to have peers like himself with whom he can exchange ideas and partner in activities.

EDUCATIONAL GOALS AND OBJECTIVES

Organizational skills:

Goal: N shall demonstrate the ability to complete daily and long term assignments with 80% accuracy. (NOTE: This is an organizational area of instruction and not one for written language.)

Objectives:
1. N shall enter all long and short term assignments on his APP "The Reminder" (Apple Ipad), with specific due dates and requirements for the work .
2. He will program the Alert signal to remind him when the work is due, and check completion circle when work is finished.
3. He will verbalize to the appropriate adult/software the sequential steps needed in order to complete the assignment. It will be acceptable if he skips steps if in doing so he achieves the same result with the same degree of accuracy.
4. He will verbally ask the teacher as needed for clarification and/or input on how to complete/organize the assignment after, or before class, or by email.
5. He will maintain a 3 ring binder with sections for long and short term assignments, classroom notes and handouts, all of which may be color coded as needed.

Written Expressive Language

Goal: N shall demonstrate improved writing mechanics through use of computer technology with 100% accuracy.

Objectives:
1. He shall utilize spell check in written classroom work (with print out ability) to prevent spelling errors.
2. He shall demonstrate improved grammar mechanics, including run-on sentences through use of "Grammar Daily" APP (Apple ipad).
3. He shall add detail to his expanded written work to a minimum of three paragraphs, including topic sentence, development, and conclusion/transition sentence. This will include the four sentence types (declarative, interrogative, imperative, exclamatory) and a variety of sentence structures (compound, compound complex, etc.)

Computer Technology

Goal: N shall utilize his computer and software appropriately in each class to complete the writing requirements 90% of the time.

Objectives:
1. He shall use "Notes Plus" APP (ipad Apple) to take classroom notes.
2. He shall use Dragon Naturally Speaking as voice activated software to complete written assignments.
3. He shall review the printout out of Dragon Naturally Speaking and be able to explain the punctuation, sentence structures and parts of speech upon request.

<u>Self-regulation</u>
Goal: N shall develop and maintain behaviors to assist him in school so that his obsession with computers is controlled and his social/emotional health is improved.

Objectives:
1. He shall inhibit his compulsion to work/play with electronics, deferring that desire for work with his mentor.
2. He shall go to bed and to sleep at an appropriate time so as to get to school on time.
3. He shall verbally identify the cause of his behavior and at least two options available to him to avoid the problem in the future.
4. He shall learn breathing techniques and other tools to self-calm when experiencing stress.
5. He shall verbally identify cause and effect in school experiences that result in his stress.
6. He shall identify when he is in error, what he did that was unacceptable, and what options he has to improve his conduct in the future.
7. He shall learn to apologize and why that is important when he has hurt or embarrassed another person.

<u>Mentorship</u>
Goal: N shall establish a friendship/mentorship with an expert in a field of interest and meet with him/her one time per week for 90 minutes per session.

Objectives:

1. He shall engage in a project of advanced learning in a field of his choice: science, computers, etc.
2. He shall choose a research project and a question to be explored, explaining why he chose it and what he wants to achieve as a result of his research.
3. He shall analyze and set down the steps to be followed in the research with the guidance of the expert.
4. He shall produce an independent project/product by the end of a semester that shows his research and be able to explain the questions and processes involved.

MODIFICATIONS AND SUPPLEMENTARY AIDS

1. No classroom work will be paper based through the end of the school year.
2. N will have his own computer and printer at a workstation in his classrooms. This will be after the staff has been in-serviced in the technology and how to work with Nico during classroom instruction.
3. Hard copy of textbooks.
4. He will be provided with praise and positive reinforcement for both his gifts and for the written work he produces.
5. Behavior and consequences will be developed with input from 4 Winds Psychiatric Hospital, and with the help of a consultant in Twice Exceptional students.
6. Modify length of assignments when there are many of the same items.
7. The mother may notify his teachers if he has difficulty with homework or a social or emotional issue that has arisen. Resolution of these problems is to be placed in writing through the end of the school year.

IEP 2

P.N., Boy, Age 17

Classification: M.D.
ADHD
Tourette Syndrome
Dyslexia
Poor social skills
Adoption issues

PRESENT LEVELS OF EDUCATIONAL PERFORMANCE

Academics

P is inconsistent in his work habits, In Woodshop he is making a chess board, with average ability using his hands and electric tools. In English, he is borderline because of failure to hand in assignments, inconsistent performance, and doing poorly on tests. In comprehension he has difficulty with chronological order, spelling, following directions, and having friends. In handwriting he only prints, his cursive writing being extremely slow. He is also borderline in Gym and frequently tardy and unprepared.

History is a favorite subject for him, particularly European. He indicates that this is due to his history of adoption. He considers himself to be good with maps and is able to do his homework independently. Science is viewed by P as "the slowest class of the day." He states there is a lot of homework, vocabulary study, written assignments, and no hands-on projects. His teacher reports that he fails to turn in assignments and they are of poor quality. He does poorly on tests and quizzes, refuses to bring his three ring notebook, and is not organized or attentive. He is failing Geometry, where he performs inconsistently. He fails to pay attention and does poorly on tests and class participation. The teacher states that he must be more attentive, better apply himself, review work at home every evening, and try harder to keep up with the class.

He has extreme subtest scatter with a subtest score of 15 in Similarities, and a 5 in Arithmetic and Coding. In local district testing, he got a zero in Pronouns, Noun, Adjectives, Library Skills and Economics. He received a 40 in Unfamilar Words in context, Multimeaning words, written forms, number sentences and ecology. He received a perfect score in sentence punctuation and multiplication of decimals and fractions..

Adaptive Behavior

P appears to display an extremely self-centered interest in his own needs to the exclusion of others, and is a very concrete thinker. He appears to have no friends in school and does not have the communication, social and interpersonal skills needed to establish and sustain a friendship. His after school time centers upon his work with the fire department. At present, he is intensely interested and involved with the fact that he is adopted, perceiving incorrectly that he is not a

U.S. citizen. This perception gives him severe anxiety. He is trying to find his biological family in Luxembourg,

P is also strongly interested in fashion and fashion design. He prides himself on liking "expensive things" and spends his own money any way he wants. He has a 16 hour per week job pumping gas for minimum wage. His main concern about school is that "Teachers talk too fast. They rush through to complete their lesson." He states that he needs to move around a lot to feel calm and is in constant motion. He appears to use verbal mediation as a strategy for self-regulation. He has had difficulties with peers and received an in-school suspension for "scuffling" with another student. He is a loner and has no peer friendships. He has befriended the school nurse because he gets stomach aches between meals. The nurse keeps a loaf of bread for him as well as Rolaids or Pepto Bismol tablets. Many of his current problems appear to result from his adjustment after leaving a private residential school for dyslexics and attending a public high school.

His classroom teacher states that P has "tremendous problems" in his social relationships. Though he began the school year showing independence, he finished it with dependence on all staff to help him. His psychiatrist states that P has a pattern of falling apart at the end of the year, seeing himself as different from other students and not being required to follow school rules. His lateness in coming to school is explained by him seeing being one minute late the same as 30 minutes late. His impulsivity is attached to his concrete thinking. He constantly wanders from class, looking for excuses to leave the classroom. His teachers initiated "Wanderless Wednesday" for him as a way to limit his absence from the classroom

He requires a great deal of 1:1 intervention for success and a great deal of quiet because of his sensitivity to sound. All curricula involving reading must be adapted, and homework, testing and grading procedures will also have to be modified. He requires maximum structure, a multi-sensory, experiential approach to learning, and use of Recordings for the Blind so that he has access to classroom content in textbooks and printed material.

Transition

P likes horseback riding, grooming horses, and knows a little first aide. He would also like to improve his typing, and study accounting and business management.

EDUCATIONAL GOALS AND OBJECTIVES

Social
Goal: P will improve his social skills.

Objectives:
1. He will seek out and maintain at least one friendship for a period of two months.
2. He will demonstrate the ability to ask socially appropriate questions of his peers 70% of the time.
3. P will show the ability to refuse an inappropriate request of a peer 70% of the time.
4. He will demonstrate the ability to listen without interrupting the speaker 70% of the time.

5. P will demonstrate the ability to inhibit talking about himself without asking questions of the listener, and wait for an answer 3 out of 5 times.
6. P will demonstrate the ability to interpret body language of others through verbal expression with 65% accuracy upon request of an authority figure.
7. P will demonstrate the ability to talk on the telephone at an age appropriate level, show appropriate listening skills and use socially appropriate language 65% of the time.
8. P will select an extra-curricular activity and actively participate in it throughout the upcoming school year. (Evaluative criteria: Participation in two or more school theater productions.)

Emotional

Goal: P shall demonstrate improved emotional functioning.

Objectives:
1. He will demonstrate his ability to explore issues relating to adoption through research projects, improvisations, etc. in school related assignments.
2. He will demonstrate the ability to research and seek out information about American citizenship, formulating an action list leading to his citizenship with 80% accuracy.
3. He will show willingness to explore different sides of a question through implementation of a Values Clarification program. (Evaluative criteria: Percentage of taped responses to social and moral questions.)
4. He will show the ability to remain in the classroom 70% of the time.
5. He will show the ability to complete a structured task both correctly and independently 75% of the time.
6. He will get to school on time 95% of the time.
7. He will demonstrate an understanding of and the basis for school rules with 90% accuracy.
8. He will demonstrate that he is required to follow school rules 80% of the time.

Grammar

Goal: P shall demonstrate improved written grammar.

Objectives:
1. He will auditorally master the concept of prefix, root, and suffix with 70% accuracy.
2. He will visually master the concept of prefix, root, and suffix with 70% accuracy.
3. He will conceptually master noun, pronoun and adjective recognition with 70% accuracy.
4. He will identify with 65% accuracy the nouns, pronouns and adjectives in reading from across content areas.

Written expressive language

Goal: P shall improve his written language.

Objectives:

1. He will orally develop and tape record examples of a paragraph with 70% accuracy.
2. He will orally identify the topic sentence in that paragraph with 70% accuracy.
3. He will write his paragraph from the tape recording with 65% accuracy in punctuation and spelling.
4. He will underline the topic sentence with 65% accuracy.
5. He will orally identify and distinguish between a general idea and a specific idea with 65% accuracy.
6. He will make a categorical heading from content related areas, making lists of no more than five details under those headings with 70% accuracy.
7. He will develop his lists in #6 above into written paragraphs with 70% accuracy.

Library

Goal: P shall indicate improved library skills.

Objectives:
1. P will demonstrate the ability to use the computer to find topics and their subheadings with 90% accuracy.
2. He will demonstrate understanding of three different reference sources with 90% accuracy.

Study Skills

Goal: P shall demonstrate improved study skills.

Objectives:
1. He will show the ability to organize his physical supplies and materials before beginning to study/do homework 75% of the time.
2. He will list in priority order what must be done on a nightly and weekly basis in all subjects 75% of the time.
3. He will demonstrate the ability to meet his homework deadlines with 70% accuracy.

Auditory training

Goal: P shall improve his listening skills.

Objectives:
1. He will perceive and process the whole word, sentence or story when given partial information 65% of the time.
2. He will recognize errors in pronunciation of words 90% of the time.
3. He will synthesize isolated sounds into words 70% of the time.
4. He will recognize the correct form of words (singular, plural, possessive, homonym, etc.) through contextual cues 50% of the time.

Visual training

Goal: P shall improve his visual processing.

Objectives:
1. He will classify concepts presented visually with 90% accuracy.
2. He will understand and follow visual directions with 90% accuracy.
3. He will demonstrate understanding of cause and effect with 80% accuracy.
4. He will predict outcomes or anticipate what will happen next when presented with visual representations 80% of the time.
5. He will comprehend incongruities when presented with a visual 80% of the time.
6. He will recognize and use visual patterns in words, objects and a series with 70% accuracy.
7. He will provide alternate solutions in problem solving 50% of the time.
8. He will understand and recognize multiple meanings of words with 50% accuracy.
9. He will determine fact from fiction, relevant from irrelevant facts with 70% accuracy.

ORTHOPEDIC IMPAIRMENT

This means a severe orthopedic impairment that adversely affects a child's educational performance. The term includes impairments caused by a congenital anomaly, impairments caused by disease (e.g., poliomyelitis, bone tuberculosis), and impairments from other causes (e.g., cerebral palsy, amputations, and fractures or burns that cause contractures.)

Sensory integration dysfunction is to the brain what indigestion is to the digestive tract. The word dysfunction is the same as malfunction; it means that the brain is not functioning in a natural, efficient manner. Sensory means that the inefficiency of the brain particularly affects the sensory systems. The brain is not processing or organizing the flow of sensory impulses in a manner that gives the individual good, precise information about himself or his world. When the brain is not processing sensory input well, it usually is also not directing behavior effectively. Without good sensory integration, learning is difficult and the individual often feels uncomfortable about himself, and cannot easily cope with ordinary demands and stress.

(Ayres)

IEP 1

K.S., Girl, Age 10

Classification: Orthopedically handicapped
Nonambulatory
Head brace
Intellectually gifted

Note: The issue in dispute in this IEP was the school's refusal to let the student use her motorized wheel chair within the school building.

PRESENT LEVELS OF EDUCATIONAL PERFORMANCE

K is a student with superior intelligence as measured by the last triannual assessments. Her medical status is fragile and she is in a wheel chair. She presently receives only 2 ½ hours of school per day. Her schedule at the present time is:

A.M.

8:00-9:00	Waking and breakfast
9:15-10:45	Exercises/Therapies
10:45- 11:15	Washing/Dressing
11:15- 12:00	Lunch/Story

P.M.

12:10- 12:20	Transportation to school
12:20- 2:55	School
2:55- 3:15	School pick-up
3:15- 3:45	Snack/Free time
3:45- 4:45	Socialization/Play time
5:00- 6:00	Dinner
6:00- 7:30	Family time
7:30- 8:00	Get ready for bed
8:00	Bedtime

K's mother provides 50% of the individualized services K requires in order to function academically, socially and emotionally. These include 90 minutes of multiple daily therapies, and socialization experiences about stories and discussions on a variety of topics. The mother has lupus, requiring medication, and is cautioned not to over exert herself in any way. In addition to providing K with therapies, the mother also provides transportation to and from school, as well as functioning as the substitute 1-1 aide when the school aide is absent.

K presents a keen interest in learning and is eager to go to school and do school-related activities at home. She has not been evaluated academically in several years. Her teacher and aide will provide their input regarding her strengths and weaknesses in the classroom. Her academic achievement thus far is all As, with only a few Bs. Her adaptive behavior includes shyness and withdrawal in new situations. She

100

requires emotional support and assistance from others. K accepts her disability, but questions whether or not school personnel accept her in the same way they would a non-disabled student. She is an observer, assessing the situation and people involved before engaging in conversation. When familiar with the situation, she is sociable and an excellent conversationalist.

K's personal and social development is inextricably linked with her severe handicaps. She is totally dependent on others, except when using her "Hot Wheels", a motorized wheel chair which she can self-direct and propel. With her Hot Wheels, she can play outside with neighborhood children, and engage in games and play activities with parental supervision. Inside, play activities take place independently. The key to her independent functioning, then, is the ongoing use of her Hot Wheels. Without this motorized wheel chair she has been a social isolate, interacting only with her family and one friend that she frequently invites to her home. She often asks why she is not invited to other children's houses to play.

K is very language proficient, her communication style usually reticent. Her physical education needs require extensive adaptation including a review of the current physical education curriculum. She has no formalized outside recreational activities. Her primary source for both nurture and support is her mother. Her self-help skills include being able to feed herself the majority of the time. It is to be noted that her head is in a brace so that her field of vision is also fixed.

Access for K requires a room temperature between 70-75 degrees within her educational environment. Therefore, all classrooms in which her education occurs must be maintained at that temperature. Physical access requires both curb-cuts and ramps. Additional issues such as toileting, doorknobs, handles, etc. must also be considered and accommodations reached.

EDUCATIONAL GOALS AND OBJECTIVES

Independence

Goal: K shall demonstrate increased independence and self-sufficiency.

Objectives:
1. K shall travel from class to class without the help of an aide 60% of the time.
2. She shall participate in playground and classroom activities when appropriate 80% of the time.
3. She shall verbalize her wants and needs within the school setting without cuing 70% of the time.

Self confidence

Goal: K shall demonstrate increased self-esteem and self-confidence.

Objectives:
1. K shall increase participation in classroom free play 60% of the time.
2. She will successfully complete such helping tasks as flag leader, messenger, etc. 80% of the time.
3. She will verbalize and share feelings and experiences with her peers as appropriate 80% of the time.

Goal: K shall demonstrate awareness of her physical needs to others.

Objectives:
1. She will ask for teacher assistance when her vision and hearing are obstructed 80% of the time.
2. She will verbalize when the room is too hot or cold 90% of the time.
3. She will ask for help from the classroom teacher when needed 80% of the time.
4. She shall verbalize to her teacher or aide when she feels physical discomfort 80% of the time.

Fine motor skills
Goal: K shall demonstrate growth in her fine motor skills.

Objectives:
1. She shall demonstrate production of handwriting and tracing to a 4.6 age level 70% of the time.
2. She shall demonstrate introductory skills with both compute and word processor.
3. She will show the ability to use voice activated software for completion of her writing assignments 70% of the time.

Physical activities
Goal: K shall demonstrate participation in appropriate physical activities.

Objectives:
1. She shall participate in relay races using her Hot Wheels 60% of the time.
2. She will participate in structured/unstructured activities as requested by the teacher 70% of the time.
3. She will comply with rules established by school authorities regarding use of her Hot Wheels both in school and on school property 90% of the time.

Music
Goal: K shall participate in music activities.

Objectives:
1. She will demonstrate the ability to sing with her peers in school-based music activities 80% of the time.
2. She will demonstrate the ability to play jointly selected rhythm instruments 70% of the time.

NOTE: Remaining goals and objectives for the IEP are to be completed by the physical and occupational therapist and put in the instructional portion of this IEP.

Related Services:
O.T. 1 hour, 1-1, 5 days per week, at home
P.T., 1 hour, 1-1, 5 days per week, at home
Transportation of electric wheel chair to/from school

1-1 personal aide, jointly selected by the school and parent
Mechanical engineer to evaluate the BTUs of the air conditioners to be used relevant to room variables
Extended school year

Modifications and accommodations

K requires a full day of specialized instruction in order to meet her unique needs. She is to receive her related services five times a week, for 45 minutes in both O.T. and P.T. in the morning at home through itinerant specialists. She shall participate in the regular First Grade program in the afternoon with a 1-1 personal aide. All classrooms, except the gym, shall be provided with an air conditioner so that temperature is maintained between 65-75 degrees. Both teaching staff and peers shall receive in-service training and instruction from the therapists, mother, and medical doctor about K's status and how she is to be treated within the classroom. In addition:

1. All physical equipment needed by K shall be on site and ordered in June for the following school year.

2. Strategies shall be developed for the 1-1 aide by parent, school nurse, and teacher in order to minimize impact upon K's socialization.

3. A meeting shall occur one week before the first day of school between the classroom teacher and aide to coordinate activities and enhance K's classroom integration.

4. K's electric wheel chair shall be transported to school daily by school van in accordance with the supplier's safety requirements.

5. The school nurse shall notify the mother if the school building temperature is not appropriate so that alternative plans can take place [prior to K's arrival at school.

6. Barrier free issues shall be evaluated within the first 2 weeks of the school year, addressed, and monitored on an ongoing basis.

7. Teacher and aide shall be highly sensitive to the fact that K cannot move her head and has a restricted field of vision. All blackboard and lecture type of activities need to be considered with this in mind. Adaptations shall occur through use of the 1-1 aide, as well as appropriate positioning.

8. K may use magic markers in class as an alternative/substitute for a pen/pencil at the discretion of the teacher.

9. During inclement weather, K shall be dropped off at the side door ramp of the school. Plans are to be in place to have that door open on those days.

IEP 2

Z.R., Girl, Age 17

Classification: Orthopedically Impaired
Cerebral Palsy
Poor writing skills
Learning disabilities
No friends or socialization
No transition plan

CHUNKING THE DATA

Strengths	Report	Deficits
	Tutors	
Motivation		Poor dictionary skills
Desire to learn		Difficulty w/ using guidewords
Intelligence		Alphabetizing to 2nd 3rd letter
Good calculator skills		Reading skills
		Difficulty w/segmentation
		Slow reading rate
		Retelling/rephrasing
		Summarizing
		Application of prefix/root/suffix
		Use of decoding skills
		Outlining
		Little concept of purpose
		Outlining forms
		Poor self-image
		Concerned about health/fatigue
		Overwhelmed w/amount of homework
		Worried about her future
		Does not ask for a break from work
		Visibly exhausted after 45 minutes of instruction
		Sometimes thinks she knows the answer when she doesn't
		Understanding concepts leading to answer
		Independent use of Internet
		Doing topic searches
		Using email
		Leisure time- no outside interest

Strengths	Report	Weaknesses

Medical Swallowing Evaluation

Chin tuck used to compensate

Static encephalopathy
Birth injury
Mild DD, CP, chronic VE tremor
Overall weakness
Mildly reduced lingual strength/coordination
Slow/labored chewing
Mild/moderate oro-pharyngial dysphagia
Delayed swallow reflex
Problems w/thin liquids
Mild residue of all consistencies
Swallowing therapy recommended

....

IEP Meeting Minutes

Works well w/time/space/information given in one form

Reading, writing, spelling
Lack of socialization
Rarely speaks w/other students
Often alone at lunch
Independent note taking

....

Assistive Technology Update

Worked hard/good results
Greatly improved ability w/ DNS

Editing first drafts
Outlines for pre-writing/idea organization
Typing very difficult/tiring
Collaboration needed between AT/ teachers
Summer instruction recommended
Pre-writing
First draft
Editing

....

Psycho-educational assessment

Written language, untimed, very superior
Math subtest, untimed- Average
Oral language, untimed, average
Nonverbal cognitive flexibility- high average
Cognitive Efficiency- answers accurate, untimed

Poor gross/fine motor coordination
Timed tests cause fatigue
Writing quickly impacts test results
Combined auditory/visual cues overstimulate
Very Low score resulted from timed test
Self- reliance- Clinically Significant
Low confidence level
Ability to make decisions
Solving problems
Being dependable

....

Strengths	Report	Weaknesses

Neurodevelopmental evaluation

Has laugh not seen before

On 10/100 b.i.d. Sinemet
Dysarthric speech
Hypotonia
Bradykinesia

....

Occupational therapy

Arms on table top for stability doing fine motor
Good scanning of printed page
Mostly independent in dressing
 Sweet/cooperative girl

Decreased postural stability
Fixes at many joints
Uses extreme pressure during writing tasks
Has tremors
Folding paper in half
Putting paper clip on paper
Poor eye-head convergence during tracking
Using knife to cut/spread
Unable to open combination lock

....

Z's Transition Concerns

School
Handwriting homework
Geometry
Concerned about travel to/from college
No experience using public transportation
No friends

Barriers for successful employment
Fine motor skills
Oral/written communication skills
Interpersonal skills
Cognitive, quantitative, social skills
Reading, writing, comprehension
Spelling/grammar

Instruction needed for independent living
Clothing care
Meal preparation/nutrition/organizational skills
Household management, money management/checking
Hygiene/grooming/self-advocacy
Health/first aid, safety/interpersonal skills
Transportation/mobility skills, community awareness
Consumer skills, time management
Parenting/child development

Strengths, Special Interests, Preferences

Z's strengths are in her intelligence, academic motivation, diligence, and work ethic. In spite of her concern about her physical strength and status, she perseveres to meet unmodified course requirements. At home she enjoys computer games and watching TV. As she enters her senior year she does not know what field to pursue in postsecondary education.

Interfering with her achievement in the General Education program is:

Any activity involving writing
Any sequencing activity
Lack of self-confidence
Completion of timed tasks
Refusal to participate in extra-curricular activities
Verbal intelligibility
Poor self-advocacy skills
Fatigue

Activities involving fine/gross motor competence
Slow work style
Social isolation
Swallowing
Independence
Distracted by multi-modal input
Lack of computer/AT skills in classes

Parental Concerns

Parents are concerned about Z's readiness for post-secondary education and employment. A primary issue is the unresolved use of assistive technology and appropriate software, its infusion into her regular education classes, and her complete reliance upon her aide to take notes. The parents have scheduled a comprehensive AT (Assistive Technology) evaluation at Boston Children's Hospital in order to better understand how to address her writing needs. They believe that she is a bright student who has not been given the proper supports to demonstrate her potential. They question the legitimacy of the A and B letter grades she has received throughout high school. In addition they have expressed concern about her social isolation, her passivity, and her delayed social development and interest in the world outside of school and home, as well as her need for instruction in certain activities of daily living.

PRESENT LEVELS OF EDUCATIONAL PERFORMANCE

Currently Z is enrolled in all general education classes, with the support of Study Skills. She receives speech therapy once a week and is trained on Dragon Naturally Speaking once monthly. She received this instruction and use of assistive technology in order to meet her writing-related IEP goals and objectives. The most recent updates note good progress with the need to receive summer instruction and better classroom integration. Her 1-1 aide takes all of her notes during classroom instruction, no computer or AT utilized for this purpose. Z spends hours nightly doing homework in order to keep up with her regular education instruction and has requested tutoring help in both Reading and Geometry.

Socially and emotionally, she lags far behind her chronological peers, her self -confidence in the "Clinically Significant" range. She usually eats lunch by herself, is profoundly passive, and does not advocate on her own behalf. She has no friends and no social life after school. She appears to have no "street smarts" and is vulnerable to experiences she will face after graduation. Her social adjustment and adaptive behavior are concerns of both school and parents.

Current academic testing shows her skills to range from Very Superior to Average on untimed tests. The untimed scores are viewed as the accurate measure of her abilities. She has several difficulties in reading, including decoding and segmentation. Her vocabulary skills are weakened due to lack of practice in higher level thinking skills and use in conversation. Dictionary skills are also far below what is needed for independence. She has difficulties in finding and applying guidewords and alphabetizing to the 3rd and 4th letter of words. Outlining as a study tool is unknown to her. She finds summarizing and restating very difficult and neither understands the purpose nor forms of an outline. She uses a calculator in math, the language and vocabulary of Geometry very difficult for her. She is often able to get the correct answer via calculator without knowing the applicable concepts. It is vital that instruction be provided through only one modality at a time, multi-modal presentations leading her to become distracted and overwhelmed.

Physical and Health Status

Z has a swallowing disorder so that food accumulates in her mouth. This also affects the placement of her jaw, causing her mouth to open inappropriately. She has bradykinesia, treated with 50/200 b.i.d. of Sinemet CR, and hypotonia with some dystonic hand movements. She is physically small and fatigues easily, and has difficulty using a knife to cut and spread food. She has poor eye-head convergence during tracking, and cannot open her locker.

Include other educational needs that result from the student's disability

Z requires assistive technology as an integral part of her academic instruction throughout the day. This includes use of the Internet for research and general information purposes, as well as the use of email. In addition she requires intensive developmental and functional instruction in socialization, self-advocacy, reading body language of situations, human sexuality, and use of public transportation. Her communication skills need improvement. She requires instruction in decision-making, interviewing, job or school applications, household management, consumer skills, money management/checking, time management, clothing care, meal preparation and nutrition, community awareness and safety.

Describe any options considered and the reasons those options were rejected.

The parent input has been discounted as "useless" by the school district.

Describe the procedures, tests, records or reports and factors used in determining the proposed action.

The IEP is based upon the untimed results of testing, showing Z's intellectual abilities. She needs a longer school day, with breaks during the day due to her fatigue, as well as remediation and socialization. Because of the complete social isolation and lack of initiation on her part, intensive counseling and 1-1 instruction after school are also required in order to meet her functional and developmental needs.

Classroom Modifications

Teachers will modify the amount of written homework assigned to Z. If she demonstrates understanding of the concept, she will be exempt from completing all aspects of the homework by joint agreement of herself and her teacher. Grading will also be modified to reflect when work is done by Z's aide versus her independently completed work. All work requirements are to be untimed, so that she is not penalized for her disability. Effort will be made to stagger the writing assignments by her content teachers. If she participates in gym, a specific set of modifications are to be added to this IEP to reflect her unique needs in that mainstreamed activity.

EDUCATIONAL GOALS AND OBJECTIVES

Academics:

Goal: Z shall demonstrate improved reading skills.

Objectives:
1. She shall demonstrate mastery of decoding skills w/o prompt 90% of the time.
2. She shall demonstrate the ability to divide unknown words into syllables 80% of the time.
3. She shall apply concepts of prefix, root, and suffix to unknown words, demonstrating the ability to define them 75% of the time.
4. She shall demonstrate improved eye-head convergence during the tracking of sentences from "Poor" to "Moderate" 70% of the time.
5. She shall demonstrate an increased reading rate from ___ to ___, objective measurement to be provided by standardized reading rate pre and post-test.
6. She shall demonstrate the ability to summarize a written text in her own words, including accurate main idea, supporting detail, and conclusion 80% of the time.
   (NOTE: This is also an expressive language objective.)

Goal: Z shall master the use of a dictionary.

Objectives:
1. She shall be able to open the dictionary to the approximate correct letter section 100% of the time.
2. She shall master the use of guidewords in finding the word being sought.
3. She shall master the ability to independently alphabetize to the 3rd letter of a word.

Goal: Z shall demonstrate the ability to outline w/o prompt.

Objectives:
1. She shall demonstrate the ability to identify the main topic of the information being outlined with 80% accuracy.
2. She shall identify the subtopics in her own words with correct outline form.
3. She shall list the important details of the subtopics 75% of the time.

Goal: Z shall demonstrate improved math skills with word problems.

Objectives:
1. Z shall identify vocabulary words of the math problem she does not understand 100 % of the time.
2. She shall demonstrate understanding of the math concept by restating it in her own words.
3. She shall inquire of her instructor as to any Algebra concept/calculation she does not understand, rephrasing the explanation in her own words 80% of the time.

Computer use

Goal: Z shall demonstrate the ability to use the Internet.

Objectives:
1. She shall Google a topic, skimming search results, open and print relevant documents w/o help 90% of the time.
2. She shall demonstrate the ability to communicate to others through the use of email at least one time per week.
3. She shall demonstrate the ability to use MapQuest to seek directions 100% of the time.

Goal: Z shall demonstrate the ability to use her computer and software to take classroom lecture notes. (NOTE: This goal will specify the recommended software once the Children's Hospital assistive technology evaluation report is completed.)

Objectives:
1. Z shall begin to take her own notes 10% of the time.
2. Z shall demonstrate the use of a back-up note-taking system, such as a tape- recorder.

Goal: Z shall be able to write her own assignments, including research papers.

Objectives:
1. She shall be able to independently complete a one-page essay.
2. She shall be able to edit that one page product with proper punctuation and spelling 80% of the time.
3. She shall demonstrate the ability to dictate a 4- page report into her voice-activated system.
4. She shall be able to describe to the appropriate person any specific problems she has with either the software or the computer 100 % of the time.
5. She shall demonstrate awareness as to her fatigue, and take breaks between writing sessions.

Social/Emotional

Goal: Z shall demonstrate awareness/enjoyment of her strengths.

Objectives:
1. She shall demonstrate the ability to draw limits with teachers/significant others in her life if she is too tired to complete a task 80% of the time.
2. She shall identify at least 10 things about herself that she views as strengths.
3. She will ask to have an activity modified 75% of the time if she knows it will be too tiring for her to do in its entirety.
4. She will identify one nonacademic area of interest and participate in that activity periodically throughout the school year.
5. She will use the telephone to call a family or school friend at least once weekly.

Goal: Z shall demonstrate the ability to socialize in a safe and effective manner.

Objectives:
1. Z shall demonstrate the ability to accurately read body language 80% of the time.
2. She shall select a place to eat lunch with other students 90% of the time.
3. She shall engage in appropriately initiating conversation with other students 25% of the time.
4. She shall engage in completing at least 6 "circles of communication" w/o prompt by the end of the school year.
5. She shall demonstrate the ability to verbally defend herself when needed.
6. She will be able to describe the attributes she seeks out in people before selecting them as friends.

Goal: Z shall demonstrate greater independence.

Objectives:
1. She will begin to use public transportation with assistance.
2. She will demonstrate the ability to adjust her language skills depending on the community audience, 80% of the time.
3. She will demonstrate the ability to understand budgeting, making bank deposits, writing checks, and keeping a balanced checkbook with assistance 60% of the time.
4. She shall be able to estimate the time she will require in order to travel from one place to another 75% of the time.
5. She shall be able to identify resources and organizations in her community, selecting those and act upon that choice.
6. Z shall demonstrate awareness and response to any inappropriate sexual overture made toward her.
7. She shall be able to brush her own hair.

Pre-college

Goal: Z shall demonstrate appropriate preparation for college.
Objectives:
1. Z shall complete Spanish and math classes that are required for college acceptance.
2. She will visit the campuses of Bergen Community College and Fairleigh Dickinson University (NJ Regional Centers for College Students w/ Disabilities).

3. She will take any tests required by the Disability Support Office.
4. She will explore additional colleges/programs.
5. She will name at least 2 specific areas of interest in which she would like to work/study by the end of the third marking period.
6. She shall demonstrate the ability to know she may not be prepared for college by seeking another year of education through her high school.
7. She will practice traveling to/from home to the local mall and colleges by bus w/assistance.
8. She will complete comprehensive educational speech, language and occupational therapy testing so as to have those reports available for the Disability Support programs of colleges she seeks out.

Fine Motor

Goal: Z shall improve her physical and functional skills.

Objectives:
1. She will demonstrate the use of some form of knife to cut/spread food items.
2. She will improve her handling of paper, keyboarding as needed, use of keys/locks, materials, and improved postural ability.

Oral Motor

Goal: Z shall demonstrate improved swallowing.

Objectives:
1. She shall improve her chewing from a baseline measurement,
2. She shall demonstrate increased lingual strength from a baseline measurement.
3. She shall demonstrate an improved swallowing reflex from a baseline measurement.
4. She shall demonstrate improved jaw use, demonstrated by decreased inappropriate opening of her mouth.

Expressive Language

Goal: Z shall demonstrate improved expressive language, measured by pre and post testing using a standardized instrument.

Objectives:
1. She shall show improved ability to change vocabularies and affect appropriate to classroom, social, and advocacy settings.
2. She shall demonstrate improved appropriate pitch/volume in all settings

Goal: Z shall demonstrate improved expressive language as measured against a standardized pre and post-test measurement.

Objectives:
1. Z shall appropriately use idioms in her expressive language in formal and informal settings w/o prompt 75% of the time.
2. She shall be able to explain implied meaning in oral and written language in her own words, w/o prompt, 75% of the time.
3. She shall demonstrate the understanding/use of the concept of colloquial expressions 65% of the time.
4. She shall demonstrate the understanding of cause-effect relationships/responses from peers 75% of the time.
5. She shall demonstrate the ability to modulate her voice so as to more effectively utilize her voice-activated software to complete written assignments.

OTHER HEALTH IMPAIRMENT

This means having limited strength, vitality, or alertness, including a heightened alertness to environmental stimuli. This results in limited alertness with respect to the educational environment due to chronic or acute health problems such as:

Asthma
Attention deficit disorder or attention deficit hyperactivity disorder,
Diabetes,
Epilepsy
Heart condition
Hemophilia
Lead poisoning
Leukemia
Nephritis
Rheumatic fever
Sickle cell anemia
Tourette syndrome

IEP 1

G.R., Girl, Age 13,

Classification: OHI
ADHD
Social skills
Expressive language

(Note: The following IEP was requested by a hearing officer during a hearing about private placement. Only undisputed facts were allowed to be used for the current educational status.)

Present Levels of Educational Performance

Deficit areas

Behavior	Language
Immature, acts much younger than chronological age	Excessive elaboration
Impatient	Questions/comments inappropriately timed
Incomplete, idiosyncratic statements	Almost constant verbal production
Always wants to explain information/behavior	Unsettled, anxious, fretful, responses
Frustrated when interrupted	
Egocentric language	
Hyperactive	
Calling out in class	
Projecting blame onto others	
Easily startled	
Hypersensitive to criticism	
Extremely anxious	
Constantly overwhelmed by stimuli	
Isolated/distrustful of peers	
Does not understand social interaction	
Behaviorally spirals/wide mood swings	
Overwhelmed by internal fears/thought	
Surprising gaps in factual/word knowledge	
Minor physical complaints	
No friends	
Unpredictability	

EDUCATIONAL GOALS AND OBJECTIVES

Self-regulation

Goal: G shall demonstrate increased self-control

Objectives:
1. At teacher request, G shall note and record in writing his behavior in a problem situation with 75% accuracy.
2. G shall demonstrate the ability to accurately recognize the types of situations likely to be problematic for him 3 out of 5 times.
3. With cuing, G shall demonstrate the ability to inhibit active responding in problem situations 4 out of 5 times.
4. Upon teacher request, G will orally explain the nature of the problem situation and identify at least two things that got him into trouble 3 out of 5 times.
5. G will demonstrate the ability to generate a set of oral alternative responses to avoid problem situations 80% of the time.
6. G shall identify one short term and one long term consequence of his responses with 80% accuracy.
7. G shall demonstrate the ability to engage in appropriate self-reward or self-criticism with teacher supervision 3 out of 5 times.
8. G shall demonstrate the ability to increase his patience by implementing a count system of increasing length to prolong immediate gratification 70% of the time.
9. G shall demonstrate the ability to accept blame when appropriate 3 out of 5 times.
10. G shall demonstrate the ability to appropriately accept criticism 3 out of 5 times.

Social skills

Goal: G shall develop social skills with peers.

Objectives:
1. G shall show the ability to ask a question and wait for a complete response 1 out of 5 times.
2. He will invite a peer to answer a question and wait for a complete response 2 out fo 5 times.
3. G shall not call out in class 4 out of 5 times.
4. G shall demonstrate the ability to accept blame when appropriate 3 out of 5 times.
5. G shall accept structured criticism with appropriate responses 3 out of 5 times.
6. G will show the ability to pay a compliment independently.
7. He shall demonstrate the appropriate use of: please, thank you, excuse me, and I'm sorry 90% of the time.
8. He shall show the ability to take turns 3 out of 5 times.
9. G shall show the ability to differentiate between real and imaginary threats and dangers, expressing those differences to the instructor/counselor 6 out of 10 times.

10. He shall demonstrate the ability to read body language, i.e., facial expressions, body gestures and positions and hand gestures 3 out of 5 times.
11. He shall demonstrate the ability to appropriately refuse a request 4 out of 5 times.

Expressive Language

Goal: G shall demonstrate improved precision of language.

Objectives:
1. He shall show the ability to complete a statement 4 out of 5 times.
2. He will decrease excessive elaboration of syntax by 30%.
3. He will show the ability to appropriately time his questions and comments in the classroom 3 out of 5 times.
4. He shall demonstrate less egocentric language 70% of the time.
5. He will show comprehension of self-selected vocabulary 80% of the time.

Classroom skills

Goal: G shall develop appropriate classroom learning skills.

Objectives:
1. He will demonstrate improved oral skills in self-monitoring by:
   A. Defining the problem
   B. Approaching the problem
   C. Focus on the problem
   D. Choose an answer
   E. Reinforce his actions with a copying statement or strategy
2. He shall demonstrate the ability to roll play hypothetical situations, including:
   A. You tear your pants at recess and someone is making fun of you
   B. You have difficulty with a worksheet and your friend is already finished.
   C. You are playing a new game and your friend starts to cheat.
3. G shall demonstrate the ability to generalize #1 and 32 above into the less structured settings of a playground and school complex.

SPECIFIC LEARNING DISABILITY

This means a disorder in one or more of the basic psychological processes involved in understanding or in using language, spoken or written, that may manifest itself in the imperfect ability to listen, think, speak, read, write, spell, or to do mathematical calculations, including conditions such as perceptual disabilities, brain injury, minimal brain dysfunction, dyslexia, and developmental aphasia. This does not include learning problems that are primarily the result of visual, hearing, or motor disabilities, of mental retardation, of emotional disturbance, or of environmental, cultural, or economic disadvantage. <u>Be sure to specify which specific learning disability the child has.</u>

Several different IEP samples are provided here. Often there are few, if any, numerical scores when you begin to learn to write IEPs, making measurement impossible. But in order to use the data you have, you start with what you have, requesting for numerical scores in all areas. You can estimate where you think your child is which will require that the school evaluate in order to confirm or refute your proposed outcomes. Objective measurement is imperative if the IEP is to be viable so that you know the baseline of where your child began. This is then compared with outcome at the end of the year.

IEP 1

J.T., Boy, Age 10

Classification: SLD
Dyslexia
Dysgraphia
Giftedness

PRESENT LEVELS OF EDUCATIONAL PERFORMANCE

Academic Achievement

J. is in 5th grade and participating in the gifted program with slight modifications. At the end of the last school year his reading average was 3.9 grade level, math was 4.0. spelling at second grade level. Final grades for last year were:

Reading-B
Arithmetic- B (Needs to improve number facts
Handwriting- D
English-B (Needs to improve written language)
Spelling- B- -(Needs improvement in mastery and application of basic words)
Social Studies- C+
Science- B
Art- S
Gym- B

He is satisfactory in all Character Marks except "Working to Capacity". The school thinks he is not working hard enough, while his parents believe he is working at or above capacity in the program offered to him. The areas noted as needing improvement show how hiss learning disability is displayed within the academic setting. What is not indicated is the extreme effort of this gifted boy to receive B's and C's in areas which are reading related.

Cognition

J. Has a school history of documented dyslexia which is moderately severe. There is a ten point spread between the Verbal and Performance portions of his IQ testing. He scored an 18 in Similarities and an 8 in Digit Span. His Full Scale IQ is 122, with a Verbal Score of 119 and a Performance score of 120.

Adaptive Behavior

J's interaction with his environment is characteristic of that of a gifted, learning disabled learner. He is perfectionistic and easily frustrated with academic requirements related to reading and writing. He does not understand the reason for his difficulties or the ramifications of his dyslexia. He is intellectually eager for new information and experiences, but denied access to these by virtue of the severity of his dyslexia. He does not see himself as smart, feeling trapped by frustration of the discrepancy between his potential and his present performance. He works best with a 1:1 teacher-student ratio. Outside of the school environment his present hobbies and interests are hockey, basketball, baseball, electronic games biking, as well as other sports related activities.

Language Proficiency

J. has distinctly different areas of oral language proficiency. On a conversational level he talks about his interests in an animated fashion in a well -organized way. He is very sensitive to the interaction between himself and others. However, in academics he has significant problems in word naming, and shows slow processing of the meaning of what he hears. This is well below the standard for his age. He does not do well with time pressures and lack of repetition, demonstrating exceptionality without time pressures and with repetition.

Personal/Social Development

J. has reacted to his dyslexia with significant psychosocial manifestations, including anxiety, feelings of rejection, and a depressed self-image. This leads to timid attempts at socialization and limited motivation to participate in language related activities.

Physical/Health Status

J. has no physical or health problems. He was last examined by his pediatrician and a neurologist, both of whom found him to be healthy and with a reading disability.

Strengths	Weaknesses
Understanding of categories	Upset by lack of success
Friendly/talkative	Sound/symbol relationships (decoding)
Good conversationalist	Listening to details
Persistent/effortful	Accessing words
Powerful thinking/reasoning abilities	Processing oral language
Knowledge of the social world	Unable to use phonetic approach
Puzzle assembly	Level of academic knowledge
Spatial relationships	Capacity to learn by listening
Interpreting body language	Visual motor integration
Word definitions	Copying tasks by hand
Knowledge of social rules	Need for verbal repetition
Problem solving	Sequencing auditory patterns
Good spontaneous conversation	Recall of 4 or more steps
	Remembering auditory content
	Word retrieval (content areas)
	Combining sentences into a coherent whole
	Halting/slow in oral reading
	Mechanics of calculation: measurement, multiplication, division
	Analog clock reading

<u>Goal Headings:</u>

Reading
Math
Auditory Processing
General Fund of information
Written expressive language
Sequencing
Word retrieval
Social/Emotional

EDUCATIONAL GOALS AND OBJECTIVES

Goal: J. shall demonstrate the ability to decode on a 3.0 grade level by using an analytic phonics approach with 100% accuracy.

Objectives:
1. J shall demonstrate the ability to understand the concept of phonics by providing the sound on command of each consonant of the alphabet, using a visual stimulus.
2. J. shall demonstrate the ability to provide both long and short vowel sounds on command using a visual stimulus.
3. J. shall demonstrate the ability to decode word families using a visual stimulus.
4. J. shall decode single syllable words at a 3.0 grade level.
5. J. shall demonstrate mastery of the concept of a root word at a 3.0 grade level.
6. J. shall demonstrate mastery of the concept of a prefix.
7. J. shall demonstrate the ability to manipulate simple prefixes and root words to form new combinations at a 3.0 grade level.

Goal: J. shall demonstrate 90% accuracy in the mechanics of calculation to a 5.0 grade level.

Objectives:
1. J. shall demonstrate mastery of all aspects of addition and subtraction, including both carrying and borrowing.
2. J. shall demonstrate mastery of basic measurement calculation in liquid, solid, linear, and time measurement.
3. J. shall demonstrate understanding that multiplication is fast addition, showing mastery through the 5 times table.
4. J. shall verbalize when he perceives difficulty or confusion in math and ask for help.

Handwriting

Goal: J. shall demonstrate cursive writing skills using the Zaner-Bloser technique with 80% mastery.

Objectives:
1. J. shall demonstrate improved legibility in his writing.
2. J. shall demonstrate improved fluency and automaticity in his handwriting.

NOTE: He is not to be penalized in the content areas by lowered grades for work relating to his disability. His grading standard is to be based only on mastery of content and not written classwork or homework. Hands-on projects shall be used as periodic alternatives to written assignments, in addition to oral reports. These will be tape recorded at home to replace such items as book reports, and research assignments.

Goal: J. shall demonstrate improved auditory memory to sequence a minimum of four steps.

Objectives:
1. J. shall recall a sequence of at least four meaningful and nonsense verbal patterns with 80% accuracy.
2. J. shall demonstrate the retrieval of factual information upon request 90% of the time.
3. J. shall recall and follow four step verbal directions 90% of the time.

Goal: J. shall demonstrate a sight word vocabulary of 100 words in each content area with 90% accuracy by the end of the school year.

Objectives:
1. J. shall demonstrate sight word proficiency in isolation of 50 words per month; e.g., 10 words per five content areas of Reading, English, Math, Science, and Social Studies.
2. J. shall demonstrate the ability to read the sight words of Objective #1 within a content area sentence with 90% accuracy.
3. J. shall be able to spell the sight word orally with 90% accuracy.
4. J. shall define the sight words with 100% accuracy.

NOTE: Application to the Commission for the Blind regarding his eligibility for services for free tapes and cassettes for dyslexic students shall be made immediately.

Modifications:
Teachers will provide additional time for J. to complete assignments.
Test results will be scored after extra time has been given.
The school counselor's recommendations for the teachers will be implemented throughout the school year.

Related Services:
1. 1-1 reading/language instruction shall be provided in fourt weekly, 30 minute sessions.
2. In-school counseling shall be provided for the first three months of the school year to improve J's self-image and self-esteem and to relieve his anxiety.
3. Classroom teachers shall verify that J. knows the directions for homework before he goes home.

Evaluative Criteria:
Pre and post testing in reading, math, spelling, written language and word retrieval shall take place four months and eight months into the school year.

IEP 2

K.W., Boy, Age 14

Classification: SLD
Dysgraphia
ADHD
Mood Swings
Poor organizational skills
Above average intelligence

PRESENT LEVELS OF EDUCATIONAL PERFORMANCE

Teachers point out that K has problems with any deviation from an established routine. He refuses to try a project if he perceives it to be too difficult. He has difficulty with written compositions and a very negative attitude about writing. K. has strong opinions and is not tolerant of other people's feelings. He finds it difficult to make eye contact and shows mood swings ranging from being cooperative to stubborn refusal.

His IQ testing ranges from an 18 in Mazes, 16 in Block Design, a 5 in Information and a 7 in Digit Span. He has weaknesses in short and long term auditory memory, a negative self-image, and sees himself as a "bad boy". Helping him to verbalize his feelings has been suggested. He has poor organizational skills, is resistant to accepting new learning and unable to accept change. Panic sets in with uncertainty. He works best with shared decision making and prediction of outcome. When he feels safe he gives better responses. He does not make spontaneous generalizations. His psychiatric report shows Left-Right confusion, poor fine motor coordination, poor short term memory, poor balance, and being hyper-curious and hyperactive. He is medicated with Ritalin and receives psychotherapy. He appears very bright and does very well with 1:1 attention. There is no limit to his potential and no evidence of an emotional disturbance.

Educational testing reveals that excessive time and effort are spent at board copying tasks. When directions are repeated he gives impulsive and incorrect answers. Nervous tics are noted. Visual memory without a timed motor response is above average. He is 1 ½ years below chronological age in visual motor skills. Working slowly does not compensate for his poor writing. Memory is improved with multisensory input, but he has difficulty processing linguistic material. He needs to improve capitalization, punctuation and sentence formation. He has ongoing inappropriate behavior in Science. He is capable of more work than he is completing.

EDUCATIONAL GOALS AND OBJECTIVES

Penmanship

Goal: K shall demonstrate observable improvement in penmanship.

Objectives:
1. K shall use cursive writing 100% of the time.
2. He shall increase his ease and rate of written production.
3. He shall hold his paper on the correct slant.
4. He shall hold his pen/pencil with the correct grip.
5. He shall apply even pressure throughout all writing tasks.
6. He shall produce appropriate letter shapes and sizes.

Goal: K shall improve written expressive language.

Objectives:
1. He shall demonstrate mastery of initial capitalization, commas and periods for all sentences.
2. He shall demonstrate the ability to write the four sentence types with 100% accuracy.
3. He shall demonstrate correct noun-verb-direct object relationships 100% of the time.
4. He shall demonstrate use of the simple, compound, and complex sentences with 80% accuracy.
5. He shall demonstrate how to write an outline for all written assignments with 90% accuracy.
6. He shall organize topics under appropriate categories with 90% accuracy.
7. He shall demonstrate both concept and application of topic sentence in paragraph writing.
8. He shall demonstrate the ability to write a paragraph with supporting detail and conclusion.
9. He shall self-correct his written work with 75% accuracy.

Keyboarding

Goal: K shall demonstrate keyboarding and computer skills.

Objectives:
1. He shall develop proficiency in typing and word processing skills.
2. He shall utilize Spell Check and other appropriate technology to assist him with writing tasks 90% of the time.
3. He shall transition a lap top computer into his classroom activities for use as an alternate to hand writing tasks.

Compensatory skills

Goal: He shall improve his compensatory skills.

Objectives:

1. K shall tape record all class lessons in an unobtrusive manner 100% of the time.
2. He shall study for tests by reviewing his tape recorded lectures.
3. He shall file all lessons and homework at home according to the date and topic taught.
4. He shall use word processing to edit all written assignments.
5. He shall develop and apply a color coding system in his notebook to distinguish between content areas, as well as long and short term assignments in the content areas.
6. He shall dictate board assignments into his tape recorder so that he can write them down at home or during appropriate times during the school day.
7. He shall keep and maintain a school calendar on which he marks all assignments and dates of tests.

Organizational Skills

Goal: K shall demonstrate improved organizational skills.

Objectives:

1. He shall keep and maintain an itemized checklist at home to indicate the books and supplies required for classes on a daily basis.
2. He shall independently bring all appropriate books and materials to school on a daily basis.
3. He shall keep and maintain a five major subject area notebook which is color coded for each content area.
4. He shall keep and maintain an appropriate amount of pens, pencils, paper, and other supplies within his notebook.
5. He shall keep and maintain a weekly class outline in each of the content areas, which shall be provided to him by his teachers on the previous Friday of each week.
6. He shall demonstrate the ability to mentally divide each class period into three parts: beginning, middle and end.
7. Upon request, he shall verbally identify the goal of the lesson, the explanation of the lesson, and the assigned homework.
8. He shall demonstrate the use of key words to organize content information, rather than writing full sentences.

Receptive Language

Goal: K shall demonstrate the ability to follow directions.

Objectives:

1. K shall demonstrate the ability to repeat directions out loud in his own words, given to him orally or in writing.
2. He shall demonstrate the ability to itemize and sequence directions in steps: First I do… Second I do…
3. He shall ask without prompt that directions be repeated if he did not understand them.
4. He shall develop visualizing techniques to assist him in following oral directions.

<u>Transitions</u>
Goal: K shall demonstrate improved ability to make shifts/transitions from one activity to another.

Objectives:

1. K shall demonstrate the ability to change classes with appropriate focus, attitude and behavior.
2. He shall demonstrate the ability to have one unscheduled shift in his program per week with no more than three inappropriate behaviors.
3. He shall demonstrate the ability to make two unscheduled shifts in his program with no more than three inappropriate behaviors.
4. He shall complete #3 above with no inappropriate behaviors.

<u>Time on Task</u>
Goal: K shall demonstrate extended time on task

Objectives:

1. K shall increase his time on task in classroom subject areas he enjoys to 45 minutes.
2. He shall increase time on task in subjects that are difficult for him to 30 minutes. NOTE: These objectives are not to be applied to any area of written language. Written language must be pulled out of each content area because it causes behavioral changes due to its highly charged nature for K.)
3. He shall increase his time on task in a 1-1 setting to a minimum of 60 minutes.
4. He shall increase his time on task in a small group setting (3-5 students) to 30 minutes.

<u>Memory</u>
Goal: K shall demonstrate improved short and long term memory.

Objectives:

1. K shall demonstrate the ability to play memory games of factual information, such as:
   A. My name is K and I feel happy. The next person repeats what is said, then adds how he/she feels. This game used to be called Gossip.)
   B. A small group of students competes to see how many telephone numbers can be remembered.
   C. Ingredients of a soup are read aloud. Students see how many of those can be recalled.
   D. Waiter game takes a restaurant order, and gives it back to the customer.
   E. Place pegs according to oral directions that K repeats. Ex: "Move to the right four spaces and put in the peg."
2. K shall use rhythmic beats of language to assist in memory recall.
3. K shall apply pneumonic devices to remember factual information.
4. He shall discriminate likenesses and differences in a series presented auditorally.

Independence
Goal: K shall demonstrate increased independence.

Objectives:

1. K shall demonstrate the ability to complete classwork independently.
2. He shall demonstrate the ability to seek clarification on the amount of homework and its due date.
3. He shall demonstrate the ability to ask that homework be shortened or modified if he perceived it to be too difficult or lengthy.
4. He shall complete mainstream tests in the Resource Room independently. Rules for this test-taking will be provided to him in writing and explained orally, with an opportunity to ask questions or seek modifications of testing conditions.
5. He shall complete homework independently. (Under no circumstances is the parent to complete any homework assignment. A case manager must be assigned to monitor homework amounts and completion on a daily basis.)
6. K shall remember to hand in all homework assignments with only one prompt.

Self-image
Goal: K shall demonstrate improved self-image and self-esteem

Objectives:

1. K shall increase positive statements about himself and his abilities.
2. He shall decrease self-deprecating remarks and behavior about himself.
3. He shall demonstrate an understanding that his work does not have to be perfect and that his self-worth is not tied to the perfection of his school work.
4. He shall demonstrate the ability to back down from a position or change his mind without losing face/becoming angry.

Social Skills
Goal: K shall improve peer relationships.

Objectives:
1. K will not explain his difficulty by blaming other students or teachers.
2. He will improve his social relationships within the classroom, gym, and throughout the school building with both peers and adults.
3. He will ask staff for assistance at the appropriate time, either before or after class, or during appropriate work periods in class.
4. He will seek a time-out setting or mentor to diffuse or mediate a problem, rather than escalate it.
5. He shall demonstrate the ability to accept praise.
6. He shall give praise without prompt to a peer and/or teacher.

Goal: K shall demonstrate the ability to accept his learning disability.

Objectives:
1. K shall be able to explain the terms "dysgraphia" and "learning disability" as it applies to himself.
2. He shall be able to verbalize his feelings of fear, anxiety, and frustration with his disability within an appropriate environment.
3. He shall create a set of biographies of famous and successful people who have had learning disabilities.

Related Services:

1. 1-1 instruction, 60 minutes daily, for written language and organization
2. School counseling with a male counselor.
3. In-service training of all staff who teach K on his needs, and the characteristics of bright students who have ADD and dysgraphia.

Special Considerations:

1. All homework and written assignments must be coordinated so as to prevent overload on K and his family.

2. Specific use of the Resource Room is to be be placed in writing and attached to the IEP. It is to be used to teach the writing program and to coordinate all aspects of written language from the content areas.

3. A positive behavior modification program must be uniformly implemented by all staff and administration.

4. All research and writing projects must be modified in both amount and type.

5. Grading modifications must be specifically stated on this IEP so that his grades and self-image are not penalized by his handicapping condition.

6. Highly structured book report forms are required for K to assist him in organizing information. Oral, tape recorded reports should be considered as periodic alternate forms of homework completion.

7. A status report is needed for gym. Specific strategies must be developed to assist him in dressing and undressing with more speed. Social interactions should be analyzed, as well as the motor ability to successfully complete assigned tasks.

8. All books in all subjects must be brought home. He is never to be punished by withholding a textbook for home use. The option to this is a double set of books, one kept at home and the other in school.

9. Specific information for substitute teachers must be ready at all times.

SPEECH OR LANGUAGE IMPAIRMENT

This refers to a communication disorder, such as stuttering, impaired articulation, language impairment, or a voice impairment, that adversely affects a child's educational performance.

Most people do not consider the possibility that an obviously handicapped person may also be mentally gifted...In general, expectations for achievements by handicapped individual, particularly those regarded as severely disabled, have excluded accomplishments of significant social value. Even when handicapped children have been identified as intellectually gifted, the lack of appropriate educational programs has severely limited the development of such children's potential for exceptional achievement.

(Whitmore & Maker)

IEP 1

B.L., Girl, Age 9

Classification: Communication Handicapped
Oro-motor apraxia
Above average intelligence
Auditory processing problems
Memory

PRESENT LEVELS OF EDUCATIONAL PERFORMANCE

Cognition

B. has good learning potential, her IQ scores ranging from mentally deficient to high average. It is agreed that her depressed scores are due to her disability. Her weakest areas are: verbal-social comprehension, oral arithmetic, and verbal concept formation. Strengths appear in nonverbal concept formation, specific scores presently not available. Visual motor integration speed and production was one year below her chronological age, actual performance weaker than testing indicates. She has an unusual pencil grasp, taking longer than the time given to complete her work. Difficulty is also shown in spatial organization.

Education Performance

B is in regular second grade with two periods of resource room. Her parents observe her to complete classwork at a slow pace, so that longer time is needed for her to study. She received an A in spelling, but failed both Science and Social Studies because of her inability to pass tests in their present format. She has deficits in punctuation skills and in forming alternative endings to stories. However, her written stories are excellent, showing both creativity and originality. Math basic facts appear to be mastered. Her precise reading level in reading and math are currently unknown. She has strengths in concrete reasoning, symbolic reasoning, and long term memory. She is exceptionally talented in Art. Multimodal instruction greatly improves her performance.

Communication Style

A's quantity of spontaneous speech is limited and she expresses worry about her ability to be understood. In addition to articulation difficulties, she also has receptive and expressive language problems. She has problems in sequencing, fine motor movements, intelligibility, multisyllabic words and increased volume in the classroom.

Physical and health status

A has a history of significant speech and language delay, with a diagnosis of oro-motor apraxia.

Strengths	Weaknesses
Good attention	Expressive language
Appearance	Voice Volume
Friendly	Social skills
Cooperative	Conceptual areas
Imaginative Play	Short term memory
Nonverbal areas	Auditory memory
Long term memory	Articulation
	Writing skills
	Math
	Language Arts
	Organizational skills
	Test taking
	Length of time to complete work

Goal Headings:

Expressive language
Articulation
Auditory memory
Visual memory
Handwriting skills
Math
Language arts
Organizational skills
Test taking

Expressive Language

Goal: B shall demonstrate improved expressive language. (NOTE: There are very few numerical scores in B's testing data. Therefore, the blank spaces in this proposed IEP are to be filled in with the age, percentile or developmental levels she is expected to achieve by the end of the school year by the speech pathologist and/or child study team.)

Objectives:

1. A shall demonstrate increased expressive vocabulary to a ___ age level.
2. She shall increase the length of her sentences by using complex and compound sentences as appropriate 80% of the time.
3. She shall increase verbal expression in social contexts to ___ as measured by _____.
4. She shall demonstrate the ability to use irregular past tenses of the following verbs with ___% accuracy:
    A.
    B.
    C.
    D.

5. She shall demonstrate increased use of various intonation patterns, including those for declarative, interrogative, exclamatory, and imperative sentences 80% of the time.
6. She shall maintain a conversation on a specific subject for a ___ minute interval with one peer, a small group of peers, and authority figures.
7. She shall demonstrate the ability to retrieve language and provide information when requested 3 of 5 times.
8. She shall demonstrate the ability to verbally request clarification of information presented in class without prompt when she does not understand it as measured by ___.
9. She shall express her needs and wants in both the classroom and social situations as measured by ___.

Articulation
Goal: B shall demonstrate improved articulation.

Objectives:

1. B shall demonstrate reduced error sounds of g/j, w/v and R distortion of vowels as measured by ___
2. She shall demonstrate correct production of the long vowels A, O, and OI in spontaneous speech 75% of the time.
3. She shall carry over the articulation correction from individual words to a sentence level with 60% accuracy.

Independence
Goal: B shall demonstrate increased independence in classroom functioning.

Objectives:
1. She shall demonstrate the ability to carry her daily log book between school and home 90% of the time.
2. She shall complete her homework independently on mutually agreed upon (teacher-parent) assignments 80% of the time.
3. She shall show an increasingly positive self-image as demonstrated by ___.
4. She shall demonstrate increased self-confidence by using expressive language in new situations within the school building ___% of the time.
5. She shall raise her hand in all subjects as appropriate to answer/ask questions as measured by ___.
6. She shall raise her hand and/or approach her teacher to ask for information/assistance when needed 70% of the time.
7. She shall reply to another child's initiation of conversation 50% of the time.
8. She shall initiate contact with another peer 4 out of 10 times.
9. She shall verbalize positively to an invitation to join a group an increased number of times as measured by ___.
10. She shall spontaneously join a group activity an increased number of times as measured by ___.

Math
Goal: A. shall demonstrate understanding of math concepts and computational skills to a 3.0 grade equivalent with 85% accuracy.

Objectives:

1. She shall demonstrate knowledge of multiplication and division facts to 9.
2. She shall identify and write Roman numerals to the number ___.
3. She shall demonstrate the ability to multiply and divide two digit numbers.
4. She shall demonstrate the ability to divide facts with remainders.
5. She shall demonstrate the ability to multiply and divide money problems using decimals.
6. She shall demonstrate the ability to solve word problems that use the number facts listed on objectives 1-2.

Reading Comprehension
Goal: B shall demonstrate improved reading comprehension skills to a 3.0 grade level.

Objectives:
1. She shall demonstrate the ability to sequence the events of a story with 70% accuracy.
2. B shall retell a short story in her own words with 70% accuracy.
3. She shall identify and define synonyms, antonyms, and homonyms with 85% accuracy.

Written Language
Goal: B shall demonstrate improved written language.

Objectives:
1. B shall punctuate sentences using periods, commas, quotation marks and capital letters with 80% accuracy.
2. She shall demonstrate improved letter formation when writing as measured by ___.
3. She shall demonstrate increased speed with written assignments without sacrificing quality as measured by ___.
4. She shall show spelling accuracy in written compositions 90% of the time.

Memory
Goal: B shall demonstrate improved memory.

Objectives:
1. She shall demonstrate the short term memory recall of factual information by being able to repeat it consistently five days in a row with increasing accuracy 90% of the time.
2. She shall demonstrate the ability to memorize five children's rhymes and 5 songs with 90% accuracy.
3. She shall demonstrate the recall of classroom events with 70% accuracy.
4. She shall demonstrate the knowledge and sequencing of directions for games with 90% accuracy.
5. She shall demonstrate the ability to discriminate likenesses and differences in pairs with 90% accuracy.

Goal: B shall demonstrate improved visual memory.

Objectives:
1. She shall recall sequences of visual patterns, objects, numbers, letters and symbols with 75% accuracy.
2. She shall demonstrate the ability to recall names and or placement of objects 100% of the time.
3. She shall show the ability to perceive elements which are new, missing, or out of place with 90% accuracy.
4. She shall recall and reproduce pertinent personal information with 100% accuracy.
5. She shall demonstrate the ability to recall and follow visual instruction with 100% accuracy.

Organization
Goal: B shall demonstrate improved organizational skills.

Objectives:
1. She shall know how to begin, develop and complete a classroom assignment with 80% accuracy.
2. She shall develop the ability to organize all of her school supplies on a daily basis prior to their being needed with 80% accuracy.
3. She shall demonstrate the ability to organize both long term and short term assignments on her personal calendar with 100% accuracy.

Related Services

B shall receive Speech/language therapy 3 times per week, 60 minutes per session. One shall be for articulation, the remaining two for language development.

Classroom Modifications

All tests must be modified in their administration to provide her with extra time for completion. Her needs require integration of both language, social skills, and self-image into a mainstream curriculum. Language concepts and use must be embedded into all content areas.

Evaluation measures

Valid and reliable objective measurements are needed to gather numerical baselines and projected outcomes by the end of the school year. This will include but not be limited to Zaner-Bloser measurements of handwriting.

IEP 2

J.V., Girl, Age 14

Classification: Communication Handicapped
Severe receptive/expressive language disorder
Poor memory
Low fund of general information

PRESENT LEVELS OF EDUCATIONAL PERFORMANCE

Strengths	Report	Weaknesses
	Psychoeducational	
High motivation		Frequent headaches
Astuteness in people skills		Low average IQ
Lovely personality		Is too literal/concrete
Diligent worker		Language problems
Awareness of social rules		Difficulty with concepts
Responds to visual demonstration		Abstract reasoning most severe deficit
Shows perseverance		Poor information base
Lively/appealing manner		Difficulty expressing ideas
Strong/resilient personality		Organizational problems
Concentration		Word finding problems
		Reasoning at a 5 year old level
		Poor vocabulary
		Visual/spatial perception
		VMI- 5.10 age equivalent
		Cannot reason in analytical manner
		Sequential verbal memory
		Visual/verbal association -1st grade
		Poor motor functioning
		Bilateral coordination of hands
		Decoding/comprehension- 3rd-4th grade level
		Reading issues related to language problems
		Words learned one day forgotten the next
		Spelling- 1st grade level
		Math-4th grade level
		Sacrifices her own interests to be accepted
		Understanding social situations- 5-6 age equivalent
		IQ in mentally deficient range
		27 point discrepancy between verbal/performance IQ
		Synthesizing elements
		Giving up on tests before allotted time

135

Goal Headings

Expressive language
Receptive language
Written expressive language
Abstract reasoning
Memory
Self-image
Attention

Expressive Language
Goal: J shall demonstrate the ability to rephrase.

Objectives:
1. She shall formulate and express in her own language essential information from classroom presentations with 75% accuracy.
2. She shall differentiate between essential and nonessential material presented in a variety of methods and settings.
3. She shall verbally identify the main idea and significant supporting ideas from written material with 75% accuracy.
4. She shall verbalize cause and effect in reading and observed events with 75% accuracy.
5. She shall verbally be able to compare and contrast read and observed events/information with 75% accuracy.
6. She shall verbally demonstrate the ability to summarize a story, read, observed, or experienced with 80% accuracy.
7. She shall demonstrate increased vocabulary relating to content areas as measured by oral reading, retesting, and review with 75% accuracy.

Written Expressive Language
Goal: J shall demonstrate improvement in written expressive language.

Objectives:
1. She shall demonstrate the ability to proofread her written work to a mid-4th grade level with 70% accuracy.
2. She shall compare her written product with what she intended to write, correctly adjusting for the discrepancy 70% of the time.
3. She shall demonstrate the use of visual imagery in completing writing assignments 60% of the time.
4. She shall take notes from written assignments son the board with 70% accuracy.
5. She shall take class notes from lecture with 65% accuracy.
6. She shall demonstrate the ability to apply Who, What, When, Where, Why, and How to all of her written assignments with 90% accuracy.

<u>Auditory Reception</u>
Goal: J shall improve her auditory reception (processing).

Objectives:
1. She shall follow 3 step oral directions with 65% accuracy in group settings; 80% in 1:1 instruction.
2. She shall demonstrate the ability to perceive the beginning and ending sound of a word.
3. She shall identify rhyming words with 90% accuracy.
4. She shall be able to identify adjectives with 90% accuracy.
5. She shall identify transitive/intransitive verbs with 90% accuracy.
6. She shall apply words groups (who, what, when, where, why, how) as units of thought 65% of the time.
7. She shall demonstrate the ability to organize words into specific categories (occupations, states, types of clothing, etc.)

<u>Auditory Association</u>
Goal: J shall demonstrate improvement in her auditory association.

Objectives:
1. She shall demonstrate the ability to determine same, different and opposite relationships presented auditorily.
2. She shall predict or anticipate the outcome of what will happen next in an auditory presentation/situation with 75% accuracy.
3. She shall demonstrate the ability to identify incongruities in a specified situation with 80% accuracy.
4. She shall comprehend the vocabulary of time relationships with 70% accuracy.
5. She shall demonstrate understanding of space relationships with 80% accuracy.
6. She shall derive and complete verbal analogies with 60% accuracy.
7. She shall provide alternative solutions in problem solving with 70% accuracy.
8. She shall recognize and understand multiple meanings of words with 65% accuracy.
9. She shall demonstrate the ability to distinguish fact from fiction with 70% accuracy.
10. She shall demonstrate the ability to draw inferences with 50% accuracy.
11. She shall understand and use at least five figures of speech with 80% accuracy.
12. She shall demonstrate the ability to distinguish between relevant and irrelevant ideas with70% accuracy.

<u>Auditory memory</u>

Goal: J shall improve her auditory memory

Objectives:
1. She shall demonstrate recall of meaningful verbal patterns of 3-4 words, 5-6 words, 7-8 words, 9-10 words with 100%, 90%, 80% and 70% accuracy respectively.
2. She shall develop recall of sequenced number patterns of at least four numbers.
3. She shall demonstrate short term memory to recall information at the end of a day, two days, three days and a week with 100% to 70% accuracy respectively.
4. She shall develop recall of rote memory material with 80% accuracy.

5. She shall recall verbal instructions in the order given with 80% accuracy.
6. She shall develop the ability to recall a sequence of events with 70% accuracy.
7. She shall develop the ability to discriminate small differences and likenesses in pairs presented auditorily with 70% accuracy.

Self-image
Goal: J shall improve her self-image and self-esteem.

Objectives:
1. She will not sacrifice her own interests for social acceptance by peers as measured by (agreement between parents and school team).___
2. She will not apologize for giving the wrong answers.
3. She will not "put herself down" in order to evoke sympathy.

Independence
Goal: J shall become an independent learner.

Objectives:
1. She shall apply the ability to use the bold print in the indexes of her texts for study, organizing and review purposes with 90% accuracy.
2. She shall independently diagram sentences to help herself understand the information with 90% accuracy.
3. She shall develop the ability to use appropriate strategies: visualization, rephrasing, note-taking, with 80% accuracy.
4. She shall be able to complete homework, short and long term assignments, with 90%, 80%, and 70% respectively.
5. She shall read the material once for the general idea with 90% accuracy.
6. She shall read the material twice for more details with 80% accuracy.
7. She shall independently answer the WWWWH questions with 80% accuracy.
8. She shall be able to summarize with confidence the information references in objectives 5-7 above with 75% accuracy.

Math

Goal: J shall demonstrate the ability to apply math computation to life-skills activities.

Objectives:
1. She shall demonstrate the ability to tell time to the minute with 90% accuracy.
2. She shall master the ability to make change of any coin or dollar combination up to $20.
3. She shall demonstrate mastery of liquid measurements (cup, pint, quart, gallon).
4. She shall demonstrate the ability to convert liquid measurements with 70% accuracy.
5. She shall demonstrate mastery of solid measurement (ounces, pounds)
6. She shall demonstrate the ability to convert solid measurements with 70% accuracy.
7. She shall demonstrate mastery of linear measurement (inches, feet, yard, miles, etc.).
8. She shall demonstrate the ability to convert linear measurement with 70% accuracy.

<u>General Fund of Information</u>
Goal: J shall demonstrate increased fund of general information.

Objectives:
1. She shall read selected newspaper stories daily, summarizing the information read with 70% accuracy.
2. She shall listen to one televised news program daily and summarize the information heard with 65% accuracy.
3. She shall be able to connect the events within objectives 1 and 2 above with 70% accuracy.
4. She shall be able to verbally provide the cause and effect for 1 and 2 above with 70% accuracy.
5. She shall demonstrate the ability to utilize new vocabulary words from 1 and 3 above with self-structured sentences with 65% accuracy.
6. She shall verbally demonstrate knowledge of basic ideas and events from American History with 70% accuracy.
7. She shall verbally demonstrate knowledge of basic science concepts with 65% accuracy.
8. She shall demonstrate basic cultural literacy in the following areas with 65% accuracy for each:
   Mythology and folklore
   Proverbs
   Idioms
   Fine arts
   World History to 1550
   World History since 1550
   American History to 1865
   American History since 1865
   World Politics
   American Politics
   World Geography
   Business and economics
   Earth and life sciences
   Medicine and health
   Technology

<u>Related Services</u>:
Language therapy, 1:1, 60 minutes per session, twice a week
Counseling, one session per week
Parent training/counseling, once per month

IEP 3

M.S., Boy, Age 9

Classification: Communication Handicapped
Expressive language
ADD, seizure disorder
Poor social skills
Associated learning disabilities
Special Considerations: Adoption, giftedness

PRESENT LEVELS OF EDUCATIONAL PERFORMANCE
(GE= Grade Equivalent)

Strengths	Weaknesses
Insightful, supporting family	Defeatist attitude
Musical	Likes to be "boss"
Artistic/creative	Language is too loud and too often
Independent play	Easily frustrated
Physically strong, flexible	No friends, social isolate
Very enthusiastic, involved	Trouble with changes or anything new
Math computation, problem solving-6.3 GE	Perfectionistic
Good eater	Avoids other children at recess
Sleeps well	Organizational skills
Recognizes precursors of migraine headache	Not take advantage of his assets
Accepts importance of Tegretol, Ritalin	Not understand what other children say
Kind, sensitive	Difficulty socializing with more than one child at a time
Good self-care skills	Desperate to have friends
Helps at home with chores	Overreacts to teasing
Friendly, cooperative with adults	Inability to laugh at himself
Auditory memory for numbers	Very judgmental, critical
Good delayed recall memory	Holds grudge a long time
Very good English	Recognizing social cues
Eager to learn, please parents and teachers	Initiating positive peer contacts
Superior intellectual abilities	Tolerating normal frustrations in social relationships
	Maintaining a friendship
	Verbal memory
	Consistent attention to task
	Short term verbal memory
	Not introspective
	Very slow verbal processing
	Contextual style in writing
	Word comprehension-3.5 GE
	Takes tremendous time solving verbal problems
	Vocabulary
	Immediate recall of facts, details, exact answers
	Recalling sentences verbatim
	Inattention

140

Goal Headings

Emotional
Incapable of building on success
Defeatist attitude
Not taking advantage of his strengths
Being able to laugh at himself
Very judgmental
Holds a grudge
Not introspective
Easily frustrated
Perfectionistic

Social
Likes to be "boss"
Social isolation
Avoids children at recess
Socializing with more than one child at a time
Desperate to have friends
Overreacts to teasing
Recognizing social cues
Initiating peer contact
Toleration of normal frustrations
Maintaining a friendship

Language
Volume and frequency
Not understands what other children say
Short term verbal memory
Contextual style in writing
Vocabulary
Immediate recall of facts, details, exact answers
Word comprehension
Very slow processing
Long time solving verbal problems

Organizational skills
Time on task
Inattention
Impulsivity
Excitability
Trouble with changes or new things

EDUCATIONAL GOALS AND OBJECTIVES

Social
Goal: M shall develop age appropriate social skills

Objectives:
1. M shall seek out one child with whom to socialize, demonstrating the ability to not be the "boss" as appropriate.
2. He shall permit his peer a leadership role a minimum of one time each day for no less than a 10 minute period.
3. He shall demonstrate the ability to socialize with two children, relinquishing the role of "boss" as appropriate, permitting the peers leadership roles a minimum of three times per week for a period of no less than 10 minutes.
4. He shall demonstrate the ability to join other children at recess on a daily basis, engaging in social dialogue with a classmate with a classmate without interrupting 75% of the time.
5. He shall demonstrate decreased reaction to teasing as demonstrated by _____ (CST to fill in observable action)
6. He shall demonstrate the ability to read facial expressions. Body and hand gestures with 75% accuracy.
7. He shall demonstrate basic social courtesies with his peers through utilizing verbal invitations, praise for a good effort, etc. This will include refraining from being overly solicitous with inappropriate flattery 90% of the time.
8. He shall demonstrate an understanding that he is ½ of a friendship and has a role in maintaining it.
9. He shall ask a peer to repeat a sentence her has not understood in social conversation as cued by the teacher 90% of the time. This skill is to gradually generalize to being done in social situations without cuing.

Language
Goal: M shall demonstrate improved receptive language.

Objectives:
1. He shall demonstrate an understanding and acceptance of his slower auditory processing, using compensatory strategies, such as neumonics, to assist in recall 90% of the time.
2. He shall demonstrate the ability to focus on the face of the speaker during conversation to aid in understanding output 100% of the time.

Goal: M shall demonstrate improved expressive language.

Objectives:
1. He shall demonstrate the ability to modulate his voice appropriate to the situation 75% of the time.
2. He shall demonstrate the ability to decrease his talking in class without prompt 60% of the time.
3. He shall demonstrate the ability to generalize content related vocabulary into class and social conversation 75% of the time.

4. He shall demonstrate the ability to retrieve the precise word to express his thoughts with 60% accuracy.

Written Language
Goal: M shall demonstrate improved contextual style in written language.

Objectives:

1. He shall demonstrate the ability to differentiate between main idea and supporting detail 80% of the time.
2. He shall demonstrate the ability to categorize items under appropriate headings with 100% accuracy.
3. He shall demonstrate the ability to form topic sentences from the appropriate headings with 100% accuracy.
4. He shall demonstrate the ability to develop a paragraph with supporting detail using the items within the category with 80% accuracy.
5. He shall demonstrate the ability to conclude the paragraph at #4 above with a summarizing sentence with 60% accuracy.

Organization
Goal: M shall improve his organizational ability.

Objectives:

1. He shall identify and list all homework assigned to him with cuing with 90% accuracy.
2. He shall select one homework assignment, preferably his favorite or strongest subject, and identify what must be done first, second and third, etc. to complete it.
3. He shall complete one homework assignment independently, following the organizational plan at #2 above.
4. He shall organize all of his school supplies both at the beginning and end of the school day with 90% accuracy.

Emotional
Goal: M shall demonstrate improved self-image and self-esteem.

Objectives:
1. He shall demonstrate a more positive attitude by verbalizing positive statements about himself.
2. He shall demonstrate pride in his athletic, artistic, musical and creative abilities by volunteering to participate in extra-curricular activities and teams, as well as participating in in-school related experiences.
3. He shall demonstrate the ability to tell a joke about himself in a positive way with assistance and spontaneously.
4. He shall demonstrate less judgmental behavior toward his peers as measured by _____.
5. He shall accept the concept that all things do not have to be perfect in order to be acceptable 90% of the time.

NOTE: No time on task goals and objectives are provided at this time in order to determine if this deficit will improve as a result of the implementation of this language-based program, improved social skills and self-esteem.

Related Services

A 1:1 daily language therapy session is required for the purpose of integrating his program throughout the day with pre- teaching, strategies, and monitoring provided by the therapist.

Complex behavioral processes are in fact not localized, but distributed in the brain and the contribution of each cortical zone to the organization of the whole functional system is very specific.

(Luria)

TRAUMATIC BRAIN INJURY

This means an acquired injury to the brain caused by an external physical force, resulting in total or partial functional disability or psychosocial impairment, or both, that adversely affects a child's educational performance. This applies to open or closed head injuries resulting in impairments in one or more areas, such as cognition; language; memory; attention; reasoning, abstract thinking; judgment; problem-solving; sensory, perceptual, and motor abilities; psychosocial behavior; physical functions; information processing; and speech. This does not apply to brain injuries that are congenital or degenerative, or to brain injuries induced by birth trauma.

Any derived score based on a combination of scores from two or more measures of different abilities results in loss of data. Should the levels of performance for the combined measures differ, the composite score- which will be somewhere between the highest and the lowest of the combined measures- will be misleading.

(Lezak)

IEP 1

F.S., Boy, Age 16

Classification: TBI
Closed head trauma
Post traumatic seizure disorder
History of severe learning disabilities:
Dysgraphia/dyslexia
Giftedness

PRESENT LEVELS OF EDUCATIONAL PERFORMANCE

(NOTE: The closed head trauma in this case came from a severe car accident. It added behavioral and social deficits to the history of learning disabilities and giftedness.)

F has a verbal IQ of 145 and a Performance IQ of 89, with a Full Scale IQ of 120. There is strong neurological impairment in his fine motor areas. He was placed in an enriched language program due to his giftedness, but could not complete the written requirements of that program. He showed significant social and emotional difficulties with his peers, and did not get along with more than two peers at a time. He feels that he is picked on and bullied when among larger groups of students. His severe closed head injury caused post traumatic seizure disorder resulting in increased language disturbance. He needs firmness and 1-1 attention in order to complete tasks. He has chronic fatigue and short attention span, and is unable to express himself in written form. He appears to be lethargic, with low motivation and confidence. He has a 5th grade reading level and a 3rd grade math level, with problems remembering math concepts from one day to the next. It must be recognized that his test scores may not be an accurate measurement of his ability due to his attention and focus issues. He enjoys drawing and involving himself with others who draw. He has poor organizational skills, concentration, and forgets to hand in homework.

F has had increased behavioral incidents throughout the year, many relating to his bus ride to and from school. He recently had a three day suspension for fighting with another student, with several prior altercations with other students. There is much concern over his lack of academic progress and what appears to be regression in all academic areas. His current status indicates that he requires intensive math remediation or compensatory strategies to help his memory. In order for him to benefit from specialized instruction it is evident that he needs cognitive rehabilitation within a therapeutic setting that provides counseling, academics, and parent training so that the manifestations of his closed head trauma can be addressed by those trained in this specialty. His educational setting must recognize that whatever characteristics were present before the trauma does not disappear as a result of the injury. Rather they are intensified and altered due to changes in the brain circuitry. Therefore, his dyslexia and dysgraphia remain and intensify with the additions of changed behavior and temperament. An integrated educational program with infused counseling within a small group setting is required in order to meet his special needs. Until the impact of his brain injury is reevaluated, his present levels of functioning cannot be assessed because those outcomes will reflect the impact of the injury. It is recommended that after 30 days of his placement in a cognitive rehabilitation therapy setting , his unique needs can be determined. Levels of functioning are to be assessed by nondiscriminatory methods, and an instructional program written developed by the IEP team and parents..

This status statement provided the basis for an interim residential placement so that current levels of functioning could be determined and goals and objectives written. His traumatic brain injury could not be separated from his educational needs, so that all were considered to be educational in nature,

Language has many facets- phonology, syntax, semantics, pragmatics. If we were to provide direction for the prevention and remediation of reading disabilities, we needed to pinpoint more specifically where in language the difficulties are to be found. Early in our research, we guessed that many, perhaps most, of the difficulties are in the phonological domain, and so we put our attention there. Because an alphabetic orthography represents the phonology, however approximately, that seemed a plausible guess and, therefore, the right place to start. The results of research have justified our assumption, providing evidence that deficits of phonological processing do underlie many of the difficulties that poor readers and spellers have.

(Liberman)

VISUAL IMPAIRMENT

This means impairment in vision that, even with correction, adversely affects a child's educational performance. The term includes both partial sight and blindness.

Some teachers lose faith and give up hope. Others clamor for reform. The more radical seek to change systems midstream. The more conservative pursue palliatives. Meanwhile life in the classroom marches on: There are children to teach, parents to appease, and principals to account to. They all make demands on teachers' time and energy. How to survive with dignity is not a rhetorical question for a teacher.

(Ginott)

IEP 1

B.A., Age 8, Girl

Classification: Visually impaired
Blindness
Autism
Multiple medical issues
Nonverbal

PRESENT LEVELS OF EDUCATIONAL PERFORMANCE

Strengths	Report	Weaknesses
	Psychological	

Strengths	Weaknesses
Offers affection to family	Significantly delayed social development-0-1 AE
Sits when hungry	(May be under estimate)
Emerging reciprocal interaction w/mother	Not independently use toys as intended
Shows need through actions	Taps on everything
Voice activated "thirsty"/"play" at home	Toy interest based on repetitive sensory use
Stronger receptive language	Lost w/o routine
Understands 1 step directions in context	Severely disturbed sleep
Follows some 1 step directions in novel setting	Hormonal imbalances
Unusual language responses:	Behavioral outbursts from low hormone level
Laughs at parent's jokes	Bites own hand
Listens to certain stories intently	May pinch others
Simple explanations	Craves sweets
Strong proprioceptive/vestibular play	Eating balanced diet
Enjoys exploring physical environment	Dislikes wet, mushy food except yogurt
With verbal/physical prompt, purposeful 5 minute attending	Toilet wiping
Stack rings on dowel	Pulling pants down/up at toilet
Manipulates "fidgets"	Washing hands, putting underwear on
Internally represents certain types of info	Self-help skills- 3-4 AE
Compliant for short period when not fatigued	Sensitivity to loud sounds
Spicy/crunchy food	Teeth brushing traumatic
Drinks from open cup w/spilling	Hair combing
Drinks from straw	Limited cognitive ability approx. 25 mo
Toilet trained	Autistic
Enjoys vibration, deep pressure, water play, brushing	Blind
	Screening out irrelevant stimuli
	Attending to world outside herself

Strengths	Report	Weaknesses

Educational Assessment

Strengths	Weaknesses
Identify body parts when named:	Unable to match/sort circles, squares, triangles
Back, belly, head, hand, foot	Organizational approaches for L/R; Top/Bottom
Identified shoe, spoon, glasses, fruit piece	Self-occupation skills
Uses cup/brush	Response time
Cooperative w/verbal/physical prompts	Quantity/size
Cause-effect	Nonverbal communicator
Anticipates repeated story lines	
Turns book pages	
Responds w/gesture "yes"	
Picked up dried fruit & ate	
Independently nested 4 blocks	
Anticipates daily family events	
Knows concept Up/Down	

Diagnostic Assessment

Strengths	Weaknesses
Receptive language- 22-24 mo.	Septo-optic dysplasia
Once familiar w/activity, accuracy/engagement increase	Adrenal hypofunction
Swinging/spinning on swing	Hypothyroidism
Holding things in hand:	Expressive language to 12 mo.
Soft foam balls	Self-stimming:
Behaviors improve w/sensory massage	Spinning
Attention increased as session progress	Rocking
Responds to name	Flapping
Looks for speaker in room	Tongue clicking
Distinguishes:	Bites hand when frustrated
Stop, no, bye-bye, hi, mom	Not sensitive to environmental sounds
Responds to:	Inconsistent vocalization
Give me/Give that to me	Self-stim coughing/squeals
Stand up/Sit down	No true words observed
Turn page	Sign for No
Stop	Choice making difficult
Responds to counting for transition	Mild left labial loop
Expressive language:	Independently hold cup
Natural gestures/facial expressions;	Lingual movement of Bolus
Body language	
Some approximated sign language	
Open vowel vocalizations	
Squeeze legs together =bathroom	

Strengths Continued	Report	Weaknesses
Effective yes/no		
Sign language seen:		
Give me; break; yes		
Understands object symbols		
Exposed to Braille		
Quickly learned voice output story activity (Likes sound)		
Consistently open jaw w/tongue movement		
Drinks from straw		
Finger feeds		
Eats pureed food w/ hand over hand help		
Computer as motivating activity		Nonfunctional communication system

Assistive Technology

Strengths		Weaknesses
Success if given sensory breaks		Inconsistent "No" sign
Signs More, Finished, Break, Yes		Leisure time activity
Basic cause-effect understanding		
Responsive to One Step Communicator		
Completed Intelli keys activity		

O.T. Assessment

Strengths		Weaknesses
Enjoys listening to music		Self-stimulatory body movements
Listening to stories, swinging		Sensory seeker
Mature pincer grasp w/both hands		Avoidant of light tactile input+ some auditory
Unscrews/screws objects		Needs brushing to help focus
Strings beads		Some tactile defensiveness
Releasing/placing items in basket w/prompt		Startles easily
Good hand exploration of activity		Dislikes fire drills
Able to search for lost toys		Exerts too much pressure at times
Locates toys w/feet/brings to hands		Resistant to spoon feeding
Enjoys all movement activities, especially vestibular		Stores food in mouth
Spinning in rotary fashion		Needs help w/wiping in bathroom
Named Leg, Arm, Hand, Belly, Head while being brushed		Putting shirt/pants on
Tolerant of hand under hand assistance		Craves frequent sensory breaks
Attentive to scents		
Independently found cup, brought to mouth, drank from straw		

P.T. Assessment

Strengths		Weaknesses
Functional mobility/walking skills		Monitor abnormal foot posturing
Adequate strength, balance, and endurance		

Strengths		Weaknesses

Orientation & Mobility Assessment

Strengths		Weaknesses
Receptive language		Verbal prompts needed in unfamiliar settings
Follows 1 step direction on unfamiliar route		Prompts needed for self-protection
Understands:		Needs physical cane prompts for up/down stairs
Put cane in front		Cane tends to drift/ tripping her & others
Walk around		
Find door in front		
Stop/Go		

Up/down
On your side
Travels purposefully in known environments
Localized unfamiliar voice
Some echolations to locate objects
Uses sighted guide/trailing techniques
Probes w/cane to explore
Uses cane to go around people/obstacles
Detect drop-offs at descending stairs

Health Assessments

Likes warm food

Symptoms of hypothyroid crisis:
Change in color, usually lips
Overall paleness
Less active
Sometimes a fever
May put small objects in ears
Hand flapping
Head wobbling
Weight- 97%ile
....Height-97%ile

Social Assessment

Paternal grandfather takes many afternoons per week

Severe sleep disturbance
Family in need of support
Nurse needed for transportation
Medical support needed at all times
Adequate school adaptations for VI
Staff training
Requires constant care/attention
Parents overwhelmed/exhausted
Mother in need of support/respite
Parent training
.... Increased independence at home

GOAL HEADINGS

Expressive Language
Increased response time
Improve to 24 mo.
Consistent vocalizations
Master *No* sign consistently
Portable/functional Communication system

Social skills/Play
Improve social dev. to 2-3 AE
Use named toys as intended
Use of leisure time

Sensory Integration
Tolerates food textures
Decrease: spinning/
rocking
Hand flapping
Improve toleration of light touch
Improve toleration of auditory input
Decrease startle response
Improve Focus

Behavior
Decrease hand biting/pinching

Academic
Match/sort circles/squares/triangles

ADL (Activities of Daily Living)
Generalization of skills
Parents overwhelmed/exhausted
Understanding rights re: IDEA

.

Improve L/R organization

Pulling pants up/down at toilet   Top/bottom org.
Top/bottom org.   Improve choice making
Brushing teeth   Toilet paper wiping
Hair combing
Hold cup independently
Improve spoon feeding
Putting on shirt/pants

Academic   Oral Motor
Match/sort circles, squares, triangle   Improve lingual movement of bolus

O&M   Health Needs
Decrease need for prompts in unfamiliar settings   Nurse for transportation
Improve ability for self-protection   Constant need for medical support
Decrease can prompts for going up/down stairs   Puts no foreign objects in ears
Decrease cane drift

Parent Training/Support
Generalization of skills
Parents overwhelmed/exhausted
Understanding rights re: IDEA

Goal Headings Continued

Social skills   Independent play (Leisure activity)
Use of vibrating toys
Signs/gestures for: Use of frozen water bottles
  Hello   Therapy balls
  Bye   Bouncing on spongy surface/mattress
  Please   Initiate listening to music/stories
  Thank you   Increase repertoire of self-occupation skills
  You're welcome   Use of computer
  My turn
  Your turn
Establish joint attention

Sensory integration   …...
Shall increase tolerance of food textures
Decrease sensitivity to loud sounds

Decrease tactile defensiveness
Shall demonstrate ability to calm with music/other

Activities of daily living
Appropriate toilet wiping, front to back
Independently pull pants up/down when toileting
Washing hands after toilet, eating
Independent teeth brushing
Independent hair combing
Independent use of spoon for feeding
Independent dressing:
shirt, pants, underwear, socks
Hold cup independently
Expand drinking skills:
Raise cup to mouth
Labial seal on cup

Cane Use
Shall decrease drift to __
Shall not trip self/others
Keep cane tip positioned against wall when using diagonal technique
Improve can use going up/down stairs
Grasp the cane parallel to her body 80% of the time.
Have the railing in her right hand, "grabber grip" in left.

Sorting
Shall sort circles, squares,
Triangles, textures w/ 70% accuracy.

Organization
Shall improve independent organizational
strategies for L/R; top/bottom
She shall respond to "1, 2, 3" in transitions, using
basket to release object
Use the designated place for personal belongings 60% of the time

Math
Shall demonstrate 1-1 correspondence
Shall identify quantity up to 3
Shall identify receptively/expressively Big, Small
O&M
Decrease cane prompts going up/down stairs
Improve self-protection by:
  (List objectives)
Sequence strategies to be used in unfamiliar settings

Receptive language
Shall increase rate of response time
Follow 3 step direction w/75% accuracy
Use trays/baskets for boundaries
Pre- Braille skills
Demonstrate use of Intellikeys

Cognition/Language
Using tactile information, she shall anticipate what is coming
Demonstrate understanding that specific objects = objects/events/activities/sequence
She shall accept under hand assistance in learning new skills
She shall combine sensory with literacy activities 80% of the time.
She shall demonstrate increased cause-effect relationships.

Expressive language
Develop 1 word oral responses
Develop/use signs for:
  Up, down, middle,
  Potty, All done,
  Eat, Drink, Play, Hurt (boo-boo)
  Bounce, swing, Go,
  Give me, Pull, Happy,
  Sad, Cut, Roll, Cane
Generalize object meaning into home/other setting
Demonstrate increased knowledge of vocabulary that matches materials/activities
Fine tune current signing repertoire
Learn object communication system
Increase/refine sound repertoire
She shall utilize simple voice output device
Demonstrate choice-making skills with real objects

Sequencing
Toilet sequence- pants down, wipe, pants up
Demonstrates knowledge of how activity starts/finishes
She shall accept the sensory breaks that are part of the scheduled activities of her day

Oral Motor
Improve lingual movement of bolus
Improve mouth through brushing for oral language

Parent Training
Parents shall develop strategies to help child while finding down time; develop positive coping mechanisms; clarify neglected family needs

EDUCATIONAL GOALS AND OBJECTIVES

Activities of Daily Living
Goal: B shall improve her activities of daily living to the age equivalent of 3.0.

Objectives:
1. She shall independently locate the school bathroom using appropriate cane techniques.
2. She shall independently use signs/gestures to request food/drink.
3. She shall independently locate the place for her backpack/lunch bag and cane each day before/after/during lunch.
4. She shall be able to sequence:
   A. Opening stall door
   B. Putting down cane
   C. Pulling down over pants/under pants
   D. Localizing toilet paper
      i.   Tearing paper
      ii. Folding paper
      iii. Wiping self front to back with minimal prompting
   E. Flushing toilet
   F. Pulling up over pants/under pants
   G. Finding cane

H. Independently wash/dry hands
5. B shall participate in setting the table for lunch/taking items from lunch bag and placing on table.
6. She shall independently use the spoon for self-feeding with minimal prompt.
7. She shall improve independent drinking skills by:
     A. Finding cup
     B. Raising cup to mouth
     C. Form labial seal to drink with minimal spilling.
     D. Suck from straw as appropriate
8. She shall independently prepare to brush her teeth by:
   A. Placing toothpaste on counter
   B. Opening toothpaste
   C. Independently find toothbrush
   D. Putting paste on brush with minimal assistance.
   E. Turn on water
   F. Put brush w/paste under running water
9. She shall independently brush her hair upon request
10. She shall demonstrate the ability to independently dress herself and master the sequence of:
     A. Put on underwear
     B. Put on shirt
     C. Put on over pants
     D. Put on socks
     E. Put on shoes
     F. Put on jacket

Social skills
Goal: B shall demonstrate social skills to a 2.5 AE.

Objectives:
1. She shall demonstrate interest/exploration of the physical area around her through use of appropriate cane skills combined with appropriate mobility skills.
2. B shall demonstrate the appropriate sign/gesture for "hello".
3. She shall demonstrate the appropriate sign/gesture for "bye".
4. She shall demonstrate the appropriate sign/gesture for "Please".
5. She shall demonstrate the appropriate sign/gesture for "thank you".
6. She shall demonstrate the appropriate understanding/use of "You're welcome"
7. She shall demonstrate understanding/sign for "My turn", "Your turn".
8. B shall demonstrate initiation of a joint activity using at least 2 circles of communication.
9. She shall demonstrate the ability to role-play: cooking, dressing, playing w/brother.
10. She shall select from 2 offered snack foods/ 2 drinks by pointing/ signing name of that selected, placing in front of her/eating.

Goal: B shall demonstrate the ability for independent play to a 2.5 AE.

Objectives:
1. B shall operate a CD player/audio player (provided by the Commission for the Blind) for the purpose of listening to stories/music on tape/CD.
2. B shall demonstrate the ability to choose from 2 offered activities (CD object book/computer game/sensory toy), label the toy, and play with it for at least 1 minute.
3. She shall request/seek out a vibrating toy and use appropriately for at least 15 minutes.
4. She shall sign/seek out a frozen water bottle to play with/drink during a break time.
5. She shall demonstrate a sign for "Ball" to represent the therapy ball, initiating its use during break time.
6. She shall demonstrate a sign/gesture for "computer", initiating its use during break time or free play. This will include a switch-adapted mouse from InfoGrip.
7. She shall demonstrate the ability to play early and advanced switch games at school and at home from RJCooperA.

Sensory Integration
Goal: B shall increase her integration of vestibular and proprioceptive experiences throughout the school day. (NOTE: Sensory integration is viewed as a critical aspect for self-regulation for B. Therefore, it needs to be infused throughout all areas, particularly speech and language activities. Baselines for each shall be determined at the beginning of the school year.)

Objectives:
1. B shall expand her acceptance of food textures in her mouth to include at least 2 additional textures.
2. She shall gesture when a sound is "too loud', signaling to "turn it down".
3. She shall demonstrate decreased tactile defensiveness.
4. She shall demonstrate the ability to self-calm with music, water play, and other SI materials. Self-calming shall also utilize gestures, sign, and pre-Braille as appropriate in the stability of her behavior as a crucial foundation for learning.

Cognition/Language
Goal: B shall improve her cognition/language skills to a 3.0 AE.

Objectives:
1. She shall demonstrate knowledge of smaller body parts: fingers, chin, elbow, toes
2. She shall explore/examine story boxes (3D object books) as a story is read.
3. She shall utilize a symbol board or pre-Braille material to name one thing from the story.
4. She shall expand her knowledge of cause-effect to at least 10 items by June.
5. She shall demonstrate the ability to match sensory experiences with language 80% of the time.
6. She shall accept under hand assistance in learning new skills 80% of the time.
7. She shall demonstrate basic understanding of Form/Function with at least 10 different objects without prompt 60% of the time.
8. Through the use of tactile/sensory information, B shall demonstrate the ability to anticipate what is coming.
9. She shall use the computer program, Nouns and Sounds from Laureate Learning Systems, to increase her receptive language.

Cane Use

Goal: B shall demonstrate improved cane use.

Objectives:

1. She shall hold cane in her left hand, keeping cane tip against wall when using diagonal technique 65% of the time.
2. She shall complete all cane travel tasks through appropriate responses to verbal/physical prompts. (NOTE: A baseline list of cane skills are to be attached to this IEP by the end of September for the purpose of post-test measurement in June.)
3. B shall integrate a language system (signs/ other) to seek clarification as to travel destination.
4. She shall grasp cane parallel to her body when going up and down stairs 80% of the time.

Math

Goal: B shall improve math skills to a 2.5 AE.

Objectives:

1. She shall demonstrate mastery of 1-1 correspondence.
2. She shall demonstrate the ability to count items up to 3 with 75% accuracy.
3. She shall count to 5 sequentially, using her fingers to sign the amount.
4. She shall conceptualize the amount of 5 by touching/counting 5 objects upon request with 60% accuracy.
5. She shall receptively/expressively identify:
   Big-Small, 1-1 correspondence to 2

IEP 2

L.J., Girl, Age 10
Classification: Visually Impaired

NOTE: The following IEP was written as the result of a court order concerning the child's school program. Much important data was missing, the IEP in dispute between the parent and school being purely academic, without instruction relating to blindness or social and emotional needs. I was asked to write behavioral and social goals to reflect the parent's request for instruction to remediate social and emotional deficits. Notations in the following IEP refer to the Commission for the Blind, who was to assist in developing academic goals in conjunction with the parent, pupil and school district.

PRESENT LEVELS OF EDUCATIONAL PERFORMANCE

Cognition

The last IQ testing was done four years ago. At that time L demonstrated above average intelligence in the Similarities subtest, average ability in Information, Vocabulary and Comprehension. Significant deficits were in Arithmetic and Digit Span. Current testing shows a five point drop in Vocabulary, which is statistically significant.

Educationally, L.J.'s weaknesses were in visual discrimination, visual motor integration, handwriting, balance, gross motor, and arithmetic. Strengths were in visual memory, auditory discrimination, auditory short term memory, abstract thinking, reading, spelling, and oral and silent reading comprehension. The Associated Services for the Blind recommended the following battery for her educational assessment:
WISC Verbal Scale
WRAT in large print:
    Spelling
    Word recognition
    Arithmetic
Gilmore Oral Reading Test
Form boards for informal assessment of shape discrimination
Interest Inventory
Personality measure, such as Incomplete Sentences

Social/Emotional Functioning

Over time, L.J. had had significant difficulty in dealing with her blindness. She is perfectionistic and will drive herself far more than she should in order to achieve the same results as a nondisabled person. She cannot accept the limitations placed upon her by her disability, and becomes very frustrated, angry, and self-abusive. She has hit herself, pulled out her hair, bitten her arms, and scratched her body as reactions to her frustration. She states that she wishes she were dead, concern now raised at the potential for suicidal tendencies in future years. She has a long history of inability to deal socially with peers and is presently a loner. She does not have any circle of friends, now the only blind person within a school of all nondisabled students. Periodic referrals for counseling at parent expense had been made by the school. Therapy for the purpose of gaining insight into her feelings, and to assist her in developing an identity, is seen as the primary need at this time.

Medical

L.J. is both blind and neurologically impaired with extreme photosensitivity, low visual acuity, fidgetiness of posture, and greater left posturing of fingers than in the right hand. There is evidence of optic nerve dysplasia and a static extrapyramidal syndrome. Occupational therapy is recommended three times weekly in addition to counseling 4 days a week.

Life Skills

During the past school year the life skills needed in school were: Using a cane appropriately in the hall for independent travel, completion of homework, ability to effectively use a talking watch, eating skills, and self-advocacy in all areas relating to her blindness and coordination problems. Life skills needed beyond the school day include those in self-care, cooking, cleaning, shopping, socialization, effective use of spare time, orientation and mobility. Because of the isolation caused by her blindness, she requires weekly structured recreational experience as a part of her educational program.

EDUCATIONAL GOALS AND OBJECTIVES

Social and Emotional

Goal: L.J. shall demonstrate acceptance of her blindness and the limitations this places upon her functioning.

Objectives:
1. She shall demonstrate the ability to restrain her need for overachievement and perfectionism in all areas of her school related life.
2. She shall verbally identify those specific items and tasks in the classroom which may be difficult for her to achieve because of her handicap.
3. She shall verbally identify those items and tasks which she finds easy to accomplish and explain why they are easy for her to accomplish.
4. She shall demonstrate the ability to differentiate between those tasks which are easy and those which are difficult.
5. She shall eliminate entirely all self-abusive behaviors.
6. She shall demonstrate self-advocacy skills by seeking out a mentor to whom she can verbally express her frustrations in school on an as-needed basis.
7. She shall develop a friendship with another blind person for the purpose of self-identity, discovery, and shared experiences.

Homework

Goal: She shall demonstrate the skills with which to efficiently use the after school reader on a daily basis so that homework completion takes no more than 90 minutes per evening on average.

Objectives:
1. L.J. shall demonstrate the ability to organize assignments into long and short term assignments.
2. She shall prioritize her homework time so that short term assignments are completed first with the assistance of the reader, and that the reading component of long term assignments can be spaced appropriately.
3. She shall demonstrate the ability to independently use a tape recorder for all note taking requirements. She shall use the tape recorder with the reader on an as-needed basis so as to clarify and expedite homework requirements, as well as its use as a study aid.
4. She shall demonstrate the ability to use auditory methods of instruction and homework completion, as opposed to visual modalities, whenever she feels overwhelmed on a task. This requires that the teacher accepts a tape recording or other alternative to a handwritten assignment on a mutually agreed upon basis,

NOTE: Data must be collected on her needs in occupational therapy, arithmetic, life skills and recreation from which to develop instructional goals and objectives.

Related Services:

1. Due to the seriousness of L.J.'s emotional and social needs, she requires a minimum of two therapy sessions per week during the next six month period from a blind therapist, to be reassessed after six months.
2. Occupational therapy- 3 times weekly, frequency and duration open to change based upon further assessment.
3. Recreation once weekly with transportation provided.
4. Bi-weekly assessments as to independent living skills related to her education.
5. Monthly assessment regarding independent living skills within the home and community.
6. Written modifications to be used within the regular classroom prior to the opening of the next school year.

PRESCHOOL DISABLED

In the case of a child with a disability, aged 3-5, or, at the discretion of the State educational agency, a 2 year-old with a disability who turns 3 during the school year, the IEP Team shall consider the individualized family service plan...and is developed in accordance with IEP requirements.

Every one of the four educational foundations- development of language, curiosity, intelligence, and socialness- is at risk during the period from eight months to two years.

(White)

IEP 1

E.H., Girl, Age 4 ½
Classification: Preschool Disabled
Multiple severe disabilities
Nature of problems unknown

PRESENT LEVELS OF EDUCATIONAL PERFORMANCE

Strengths	Report	Weaknesses
	Neurological	
		Fearful
		Screaming/moaning responses
		Not imitate/repeat
		Actively jumped/hand flapped
		Suspected seizure
		Underlying encephalopathy
		Language impairment
		Possible SI dysfunction
		Possible PDD
		Constant stimulation-seeking behavior
	Developmental pediatric	
Likes 1-1		Tensing-type behavior
Walks up/down stairs w/hand		Walks aimlessly
Sits on riding toy/pushes w/feet		Will not walk w/o holding hand
Good appetite		Spaces out
Drinks from straw		Spins/mouths objects/chews clothes
References adult before engaging in behaviors		Eats sand/wood
LH dominance		Extremely upset w/transitions
Responds to limit setting		Bites when angry/frustrated
		Bottle is comfort item
		Not receive EI services due to cost
		Nuchal cord at birth/plagiocephaly
		Frustrated/bites brother
		Tantrums settle when ignored
		Too much praise= throws object
		Not affectionate
		Diminished tone/strength
		In-toes on R more than L
		Global developmental delay
		Difficult behavioral style

Strengths	Report	Weaknesses
	O.T.	
Smiled when on swing		Fine/visual motor coordination disorder
		Low muscle tone
		Somatosensory processing disorder
		Abnormalities of muscles, skeleton, CNS
		Nuchal cord pinned hand at face at birth
		Arches back when confined to chair
		Not explores toys
Explores textures w/hands		Poor strength throughout
Able to cross midline		Unable to separate head/eye movements
Makes circular scribbles		Unable to look w/diagonal/circular movements
		No sense of danger
		Pulls curtains down
		Begun to invert herself/somersaults
		Not like shaving cream
		Grasp- 1 ½ year old level
		Not imitate horizontal/vertical lines
		Following directions
		Fine motor- 15 Mo.
		Differences in SI

....

	Pediatric Audiology	
<u>Normal/near normal hearing</u>		

....

	Pediatric follow-up	
Can drink from straw		Hits chin w/hand when excited
		Not sit for meals
		Prefers soft foods/crunch cereals
		Very active
		Bolts/runs at end of session
		Jumped/flapped

....

	Speech/Language Evaluation	
Time on task- 3-5 min.		Mostly nonresponsive when spoken to
Easily separates		Not initiate interaction
Gross motor activities		Frustrated when her communication breaks down
Can attend 30 min.		Resists cuddling
Used gestures/signing		Difficult to calm
Verbalized: p, b, m, n		Avoids eye contact
Ability to request adult help		Plays w/toys in unusual manner
Initiates turn taking routines		When task imposed: 10 sec. Attention
Points to/shows objects		Unable to communicate needs
Plays Peek-a-Boo		Articulation severely delayed

Strengths	Report	Weaknesses

Speech/Language Continued

Strengths	Weaknesses
Shakes head for No	No sensitivity to other's moods
Leads caregiver to desired object	No fear of strangers
Pushes stroller/shopping cart	Pragmatics: 15-18 months
	Not imitate other children/control behavior
	Not show ability to vocalize
	Communication- 21-24 Mo.
	Not wave "hi", inconsistent w/bye"
	Not feed others; hug dolls, animals, people
	Not gesture for toileting needs
Smiles/laughs during games	Play skills- 15-18 Mo.
Rolls ball back/forth	Receptive language- 18-21 Mo.
Gestures for "up"	Tantrums to "No"
Attends to music	Expressive language- 12-15 Mo.
Responds to sounds unseen	Not imitate syllables, words, animal sounds
Stops when name called	
Sometimes follows 1 command	
Identified 3 body parts on self	
Understand approx. 100 words	
Ability to vocalize 2 syllable combination	
Squeals/vocalizes to get attention	
Says: bye-bye, dada, no, uh-oh, up, bubble.	
Shakes head for "no"	
Uses "more" sign	

....

Developmental Assessment

Strengths	Weaknesses
2.1AE Gross motor	0.11 AE Receptive Communication
	Significant deficits:
	Social, Communication,
	Motor, Cognition

....

O.T. Report Follow-up

Strengths	Weaknesses
Attempts pincer grasp	Tending to tasks she does not choose
Can scribble	Transitions
Enjoys textures/sensations on hands/arms	Limited speech
Success= being in control "of it"	Decreased activity tolerance
Seeks rougher textures during play	External/internal distractibility
Slow linear prone movement calms	High arousal level
Enjoys deep pressure input	Low frustration tolerance
Enjoys any climbing task	Self-stimulatory behaviors
Table top activity- 3-4 min.	Slight low tone in face, upper extremity/trunk
	Fair/poor upper reciprocal movement
	Unable to form shapes/letters
	Impulsive

Strengths	Report	Weaknesses
	Pediatric Follow-up	
Indicates to parents when tired		Very active
Settles independently in crib		In constant motion
Eats fruits, veggies, meats		Possible oral apraxia
Consistently turns to name		Sleep issues
Says "ah ah, out, hi		Psychosocial family stressors
Stacks 7 blocks spontaneously		
Tries toy phone only		

....

	Physical Therapy Evaluation	
Ascends stairs w/alternating pattern	Duplication of distal chromosome 16 short arm	
Catch/throw to 4/5 ft.	Static encephalopathy	
	Generalized low tone	
	Minimal/moderate weakness in all muscle groups	
	Habitually W sits	
	Moderate assistance to balance on each foot	
	Not jump down from 1 step elevation	
	No attempt to gallop	
	Awkward gait	
	Poor reciprocal arm swing when running	
	Uses single step to descend steps	
	Many self-stimulatory behaviors	
	Constant sensory input especially mouth/jaw	
	Not sensitive to auditory stimulation	
	Gross motor significantly delayed	

....

	Kennedy Krieger Institute Report	
Labels objects		Hand flapping, bruxism
Says "I want…"		Double wrapped cord across face
Refused to use PECS		Face presentation at birth
Good sleep pattern		Much cranial molding
Knows colors		Fish mouth faces
		Diffuse mild hypotonia
		Wandering/self-stimulatory behavior

....Continued to chew toy

Strengths	Report	Weaknesses
	IEP Data	
Initiates peer/teacher interactions		Intelligibility
Preschool academic skills		Toilet training at home
Plays 1-1 w/adult		Sniffing objects
Accepts textures in mouth		PICA
Mastered all learning readiness skills		Play skills w/peers/sibling

IEP Data Continued

Participates well in small groups
Sings songs w/group
Identifies colors; upper/lower case letters
Matching
Prefers art projects
Prefers playing w/balls
Listens to directions

Inappropriate hand movements
Body rocking
Chin/facial hitting
Speech output:
Final consonant deletion
Substitution b/f;n
Movement/sequencing syllables
Eye contact w/social question
Cries/bounces going from preferred activity

Parent Input

1. Geneticist said the Chrom.16 was associated with autism. Is she autistic? No records state that she is autistic. This appears to be the closest diagnosis to explain some of her behavior.
2. She seeks out water and bubbles in bath tub, etc. for immersion. Self-stims on them.
3. She has no self-care skills that generalize into the home.
4. She has no pain threshold.
5. She has chronically chapped hands, similar to father, who has same genetic defect.
6. Likes being outside.
7. Has a favorite chair she rocks in.
8. Won't drink anything w/bubbles. Uses straw.
9. Tantrums daily at school.
10. She dumps "multiples" in groups. Stims after dumping.
11. No routine after school.
12. Does board games: Candyland, I Spy Bingo, Carabou
13. Knows letters, numbers
14. Completely runs the parents, sibling; no boundaries, manipulative
15. Still drinks from bottle.
16. Home environment unbearable due to her behavior
17. ABA program not working

CURRENT IEP GOAL HEADINGS

Note: This list is to be compared with the deficit category items in the foregoing data analysis. The list below contain goal headings in the current IEP, with the number of IEP objectives now provided in parentheses. An exact 1-1 correspondence must be written in her revised IEP in order to meet all of the needs in her deficit categories.

Appropriate sitting (1)
Provide eye contact (2)
Small group learning skills (3)
Literal comprehension (3)
Sound/letter relationships (2)

Number concepts (8)
Computation skills (1)
Current IEP Headings Continued

Handwriting (2)
Cutting (5)
Gross motor object movement (3)
Aggressive behaviors to self/others (3)
Eliminate behaviors disturbing classroom (1)
Expressive language (8)
Forming questions (2)
Articulation (8)
Core curriculum G/O
OT, 3X 1-1, 30 min.
Speech 4X, 1-1, 30 min.; 1X in class consult
PT 2X, 1-1, 30 min.

Deficit Categories

Sensory Integration/OT
Low frustration
Poor/fair upper reciprocal movement
Forming shapes/letters
Weakness in all muscle groups
Hand flapping
Teeth grinding
Self-stimulatory behavior
No sense of boundaries
Constant sensory input to mouth/jaw
Oral apraxia

Time on Task
Doing tasks she doesn't choose
External/internal distractibility
High arousal level
Facial/upper trunk low tone
Impulsive
In constant motion

Gross Motor
Awkward gait
Single step stair descending
Galloping

W sits
Balance on each foot
Jumping down 1 step

DEVELOPMENTAL DATA GENERALLY FOR AGES 3-5

NOTE: Due to the confusion and disagreement between the parents and the school about the child's functioning, developmental behavior in the nondisabled was provided as a baseline, taken from Linder (1993)

1. Social-emotional development baselines:
      36+ months- Increased rough & tumble play
      Plays spontaneously with other children in complicated verbal communication
      36-48 months- Begins cooperative play; separates from parent w/o crying

Group replaces parallel play; joins other children in play
48-60 months- Talking, smiling, laughing, playing w/peers
    Group games w/simple rules;
    Strong sense of family/home
    Quotes parents as authorities
    Shows concern/sympathy for others
    Engrossed in projects
    Prefers playing w/other children than alone

2. Cognitive baselines:
36-48 months-Draws circle, face of a person; understands what happens next questions
    Sorts by one criterion w/o confusion;
    Puts graduated sizes in order
    Plans out pretend situations in advance
    Events in play sequenced into scenario
42 + months- Creates imaginary characters/dolls carry out several roles/activities,
    Directs actions of 2 dolls
48-60 months- Counts objects in sequence w/1-1 correspondence
    Puts 3 pictures in sequence to tell story,
    Knows L-R, top-bottom sequence in book reading
    Knows first, middle, last
    Counts up to 10 objects
    Knows more, less, same
    Counts objects, enumerating each object once
    Identifies names / numbers
    Matches number in set to correct number
    Understands concept of zero
    Sorts objects by size (large, medium, small)
    Sorts objects in many different ways
    Classifies into categories
    Matches/identifies basic symbols
    Identifies different coins
    Identifies L-R
    Puts together complex puzzle
    Builds elaborate block structures
    Problem solves cause-effect, representational thinking

Cognitive Baselines Continued…

Imitates scenes from life; pieces into new script
36-52 months- Understands tall, tallest, largest, short, shortest, smallest, big, little

3. Sensorimotor Development baselines:

    18- 2 ½+ years-Walks upstairs w/o support
    19- 2 ½ years- Walks downstairs w/o support
    21 months-Squats to play
    2-2 ½- Runs, whole foot contact, stops, starts; jumps from bottom step

Hops on one foot few steps; climbs up/down furniture independently
Throws ball in standing position w/o falling
2-3 years- Crayon held w/fingers, hand on top, forearm turned so thumb directed downward
2 ½ years+-Walks downstairs, alternating feet; climbs easy nursery apparatus
28 months-3 years-Walks upstairs, alternating feet
2-5 years- Jumps over objects; visually tracks ball
36-47 months- Holds paper w/one hand while writing w/other
36-59 months- Use scissors to cut paper on line
42-47 months- Cuts circle w/scissors
3-4 years- Runs around obstacles, turns corners
  Skips on one foot; throws ball using shoulder/elbow
2½-5 years-Walks w/heel to toe pattern; hops on one foot; throws, guiding ball w/fingers;
  Pencil held w/mature grasp
4-5 years- Climbs ladder

Parent Request: The goals and objectives must emphasize E.H.'s most severe areas of need, not focusing upon academics but on developmental and functional needs so that she is able to become self-sufficient and independent.

IEP 2

J.D., Boy, Age 2/12

Early Intervention
Expressive language
Low tone
No cooperative play
No transition from early intervention into a preschool handicapped class

Strengths	Report	Weaknesses
	Speech-Language Evaluation	
Sweet/friendly		Drooling
Talkative/cooperative		Open mouth posture
Expressive language-3.1AE, 70%ile; 75%ile		Identifying colors
Receptive language- 68%ile; 47%ile		Spatial concepts
		Pronouns
		Quantitative concepts
		Letter identification
		Identifying advanced body parts
		Low tone
		Tongue protrudes=excessive drooling
		Full mouth closure
		Chewing hard foods
		Drooling affects socially
		Sensory seeking behavior
		Articulation-distorted r, th, d, s

	O.T. Evaluation	
Easy interaction w/examiner		Short attention span
Followed directions w/minimal cue		Poor body/safety awareness
Responds well to verbal cues		Needs transition assistance
Identifies simple shapes/colors		Poor hand muscle strength/endurance
Stacked 9 blocks		Imitating vertical line
		Difficulty imitating age level block design
		Sensory Processing (2% of population)
		Tactile
		Taste/smell
		Movement
		Auditory Filtering
		Low energy/weak
		Visual/auditory sensitivity
		Relies on external support to keep behavior/thoughts organized
		Poor spatial organization tasks
		Only eats soft foods
		Cannot work w/background noise

Strengths	Report	Weaknesses

P.T. Evaluation

Strengths	Weaknesses
Very pleasant/cooperative	Sense of heaviness in movement quality
Runs well	Moderate bilateral foot pronation
Balance skills	Mildly decreased tone, especially core
Balance skills	Challenges w/dynamic core strength/stability
Good steering of tricycle	Frequent open mouth posture
	Maintaining balance- 33 mo.
	Locomotion- 25%ile, -20% delay
	Object manipulation- 25%ile, -20% delay
	Low muscle tone
	Difficulty w/ fatigue

....

Educational Assessment

Strengths	Weaknesses
Performs well w/adult modeling	Not play w/other children
Easily redirected	Low muscle tone
Physical development-25%ile	Tires easily
Uses pretend objects in play	Language reciprocity
Match objects by shape/color	Limited attention span
Uses 2+ word phrases	Communication- 9%ile , 22 mo.
Enjoys make believe/dressing up	Not stack 6-7 blocks
Right handed	Prefers to play by himself
Puzzles/play dough	Not throw/catch ball
	Adaptive behavior- 24 mo.

....

Social History

Strengths	Weaknesses
Happy/verbal	Very sensitive to noise
	Tolerating labels in clothes
	Prefers soft foods
	Not feel sensation of wet on his mouth
	Chews on one side of his mouth
	Dressing himself
	Tolerating socks & shoes
	Not communicate well when frustrated
	Low tone negatively impacts gross motor
	Not alternate feet when climbing stairs
	Avoids movement when feet off floor
	Tolerates only mild movement on swings
	Tires easily
	Requires multiple repetitions to grasp request
	Difficulty sharing w/other children
	Difficulty taking turns

CATEGORIES OF DEFICIT

Oral motor	Sensory Integration
Drooling	Low tone
Open mouth posture	Sensory seeking behavior
Tongue protrudes	Short attention span
Chewing hard foods	Poor body/safety awareness
	Sensory processing:
	Tactile/taste/smell
	Movement/auditory filtering
	Low energy
	Visual/auditory sensitivity
	Not work w/background noise
	Tires easily
	Tolerating labels in clothes
	Not feel wet on his mouth
	Avoids movement when feet off floor

O.T.	Pre-academics
Poor hand muscle strength	Spatial concepts
Imitating vertical line	Pronouns
Poor spatial organization	Quantitative Concepts
	Age level block design
	Multiple repetitions to grasp concept

Articulation	P.T.
Distorted r, th, d, s	Bilateral foot pronation
	Decreased core tone
	Heaviness in movement quality
	Decreased muscle tone
	Maintaining balance
	Alternate feet when climbing stairs

Social skills	Parent Note
Co-operative play	There is disagreement with P.T. report/
Language reciprocity	recommendations. Goals/objectives for
Limited attention span	all identified weaknesses are to be
Sharing	written with oral motor, sensory and play
Dressing himself	skills the focus of the IEP.
Tires easily	
May bite other children	
Frustration impacts communication	

DEVELOPMENTAL GOALS AND OBJECTIVES

<u>Sensory processing</u>
Goal: J shall demonstrate improved sensory processing to the score of 12% of the population.

Objectives:
1. J shall demonstrate increased tolerance for tactile experiences, including clothes.
2. He shall demonstrate improved arousal levels.
3. He shall demonstrate improved stamina at a task.
4. He shall demonstrate improved body/safety awareness.
5. He shall decrease sensory seeking behavior.
6. He shall improve his core strength.

<u>Oral motor</u>
Goal: J shall demonstrate improved oral motor functioning to a 3.0 AE.

Objectives:
1. He shall decrease his saliva flow.
2. He shall demonstrate the ability to swallow the saliova so that it does not interfere with ADL activities.
3. He shall demonstrate increased closed mouth posture in all settings.
4. He shall decrease his tongue protrusion.
5. He shall demonstrate the ability to chew hard foods.

<u>Gross motor</u>
Goal: He shall improve his gross motor functioning to (TBD)

Objective: He shall improve his bilateral foot pronation

PLACEMENT AND LEAST RESTRICTIVE ENVIRONMENT

You and the IEP Team have completed writing the goals, objectives, and related services. Then you ask, "Where can this program be delivered?" The answer to that becomes the named placement. Emphasis on regular education is for the purpose of bringing the disabled child as close to his community as possible, as long as the entirety of the IEP can be implemented. However, every placement in the continuum of placement options on the opposite page is considered to be least restrictive because that term is viewed from the perspective of the child and not the adult. If the IEP is implemented in its entirety, if the child is an accepted and active participant in his classroom and school, and if the education leads to independence and self-sufficiency that is the least restrictive environment for the child.

The law requires that (300.114):

1. To the maximum extent appropriate, children with disabilities, including those in public or private institutions or other care facilities, are educated with children who are not disabled.

2. Special classes, separate schooling, or other removal of children with disabilities from the regular education environment occurs only if the nature or severity of the disability is such that education in regular classes with the use of supplementary aids and services cannot be achieved satisfactorily.

3. The funding system of a state cannot result in placements that violate these requirements.

4. The placement decision-

   A. Is made by a group of people, including the parents, and other persons knowledgeable about the child, the meaning of the evaluation data, and the placement options;
   B. Is determined at least annually;
   C. Is based on the child's IEP;
   D. Is as close as possible to the child's home.

5. Unless the IEP of a child requires some other arrangement, the child is educated in the school that he or she would attend if not disabled.

6. Consideration is given to any potentially harmful effect on the child or on the quality of services he or she needs.

7. A child is not removed from education in age-appropriate regular classrooms solely because of needed modifications in the general education curriculum.

8. The child may participate with nondisabled students in extra-curricular services and activities to the maximum extent appropriate.

Every school district is required to have a continuum of placement options so that regardless of the disability or its severity there is a place in which to deliver the services defined in the IEP.

This includes regular classes, special classes, special schools, home instruction, and instruction in hospitals and institutions. It requires both day and residential placements, as well as such variations as an extended school day and a mix of vocational, college, and academic settings. The cascade of options is:

LOCAL SCHOOL CLOSEST TO HOME
Special classes, teacher training, assistive technology, classroom aide, 1-1 aide

PUBLIC SCHOOL IN THE COMMUNITY
It may be that another school within the district has a placement that can implement the IEP.

PRIVATE, APPROVED DAY PLACEMENT
Every state has a list of approved private placements. If a non-approved placement is chosen, it must be shown that no approved option can implement the IEP.

RESIDENTIAL PLACEMENT
A 24 hour placement is only selected when there is no other option for IEP implementation.

HOME INSTRUCTION
Home Instruction is considered to be the most restrictive placement because the child is isolated away from peers.

Two placement considerations always get lost in the discussion about where to implement the IEP. They are:

1. Consideration is given to any potentially harmful effect on the child;
2. Consideration is required about the quality of the services to be delivered.

Potentially harmful effect can be caused by the peer group, curriculum, teaching style, and an unlimited list of items that adversely impact upon the child's ability to learn. The quality of the service is never discussed. But that language is in the law and helps to clarify IEP implementation. The child is not entitled to the best placement. But Endrew says that the placement must provide a challenging program to meet the unique needs of the child. It must provide academic and functional development and be appropriately ambitious to meet the unique circumstances of the child. Often parents say at the IEP meeting that their child already knows many of the proposed goals and objectives. The school usually responds by saying that they want to include these areas for the purpose of mastery. Do not buy that argument. If mastery was the criterion, it should have been in the prior IEP. Make sure that the specialized instruction comes from current levels and not from the mere repetition of last year's IEP.

DON'T CHEAT
Many parents and IEP teams come to the meeting with a predetermined placement. No. Don't cheat. Follow the process and develop genuinely individualized instruction. Then follow the law, examine all of the requirements, and reach a decision. Commonly, schools will refuse to put in goals and objectives they think they are unable to meet within the district. Commonly, parents will decide on the private school they believe best suits their child's needs before ever

developing the IEP. Follow the process and only develop instruction based on data. The rest will follow.

ODDS AND ENDS

1. Private evaluations- Parents mistakenly believe that if they pay for a private assessment those findings and recommendations must be used by the school district. If the school district funds an independent evaluation, it still does not have to accept those findings. Schools must only accept the information provided by their employees. They are to consider outside results but are not bound by them.

2. Medical vs. Educational- It is not uncommon for schools to refuse to provide a service they consider to be medical and, therefore, not their financial responsibility. If the service is required in order for the child to benefit from education, the service becomes educational in nature.

3. Dyslexia and sensory integration- Two hot button areas are those of dyslexia and of sensory integration. Schools still often refuse to use the term "dyslexia". They think that this diagnosis binds them to a specific educational program. It doesn't. If the child is dyslexic, it is one of the categories of specific learning disability.. The other trigger term is sensory integration. It is a flash point because most school therapists are not sufficiently trained in treating sensory disorders. If the child's data indicates sensory integration dysfunction, then that term must be named so as to provide specificity.

4. Twice Exceptional- There are increasing numbers of classified students who are also gifted. This mix of gift and disability can be profoundly confusing to the IEP team, particularly if they have no experience with this profile. The educational needs of these students are quite different than any other population in that it is their gift that drives their development. The activities for which they have a passion cannot be taken away as punishment if behaviors and remediation are not successful. A great deal of information about this combination is available on the Internet.

5. Use of an advocate- There are many kinds of advocates. If the advocate is also an educator who is able to interpret test results and classroom performance, their presence is often helpful. However, if advocates attend the meeting as an adversary, more in the guise of an attorney, they are usually not helpful. Anyone who attends the IEP meeting must be able to contribute information about the child.

6. Child attending the meeting- Children are often invited by the school to participate in the IEP meeting. If the child is prepared to participate, his/her input ca be very valuable. However, they can often be put in the uncomfortable position of criticizing a teacher, a class, or a therapist, which should be avoided if possible. They can attend only a portion of the meeting and leave when they have completed their input. Whatever tension there may be between the IEP team and the parents, the child is to be protected from that negativity.

7. Signature- The parent does not have to sign any IEP except the initial one. It will take effect usually 15 days after the IEP meeting unless a party files for due process. Then the IEP in effect before the one in dispute continues until the dispute is resolved.

IEP MEETING CHECK LISTS

IEP PROCESS

1. My child's strengths were discussed.

2. How strengths were to be used in school was explained to me.

3. My concerns for improving his/her education were respected and acted upon.

4. I received and understood the results of the most recent testing.

5. Testing scores were explained to me in terms I understood.

6. Specific academic needs were discussed.

7. Specific functional needs were discussed.

8. Specific developmental needs were discussed.

9. Positive behavior supports and strategies were discussed.

10. Limited English proficiency was discussed.

11. Use of Braille/ or the reason not to use it was discussed.

12. All of my child's communication needs were considered.

13. Specifics of the general education curriculum at my child's grade level were discussed.

14. Extra- curricular activities were discussed.

15. I understand how my child's progress in meeting the goals and objectives will be measured.

16. I received a copy of the School Handbook/Code of Conduct.

THE WRITTEN DOCUMENT

1. All IEP instruction is in writing.

2. Present academic levels have baselines so as to project growth over the next 12 months.

3. Instruction is written for functional and/or developmental deficits.

4. There is an explanation about how my child's disability affects progress in general education.

5. All goals (and/or objectives) are measureable, stating expected growth by age, grade, percentile or developmental norm.

6. All other needs flowing from the disability are written in the IEP.

7. There is a precise explanation about how progress in the goals will be measured.

8. Specific related services, with both frequency and duration, are in writing.

9. Specific program modifications/supports for school staff are in writing.

10. Participation in extra-curricular, nonacademic activities is specified.

11. The extent the child is removed from nondisabled students is specified.

12. The IEP has specific accommodations for State and local assessments.

13. There is a reason given for exemption from State and local testing.

Transition

1. There are postsecondary goals for training, education, employment and independent living skills.

2. There are specific transition services, including courses of study.

3. The student is informed of IDEA rights one year before the age of majority

FEDERAL GUIDELINES ON INDIVIDUALIZED EDUCATION PROGRAMS (IEPs)

Interpretation of Requirements of the Individuals with Disabilities Education Act, (Appendix C, 1992)

1.

Purpose of the IEP

There are two main parts of the IEP requirement, as described in the Act and regulations:

1. The IEP meetings, where parents and school personnel jointly make decisions about an educational program for a child with a disability, and

2. The IEP document itself is a written record of the decisions reached at the meeting. The overall IEP requirement, comprised of these two parts, has a number of purposes and functions:

   a. The IEP meeting serves as a communication vehicle between parents and school personnel, and enables them, as equal participants, to jointly decide what the child's needs are, what services will be provided to meet those needs, and what the anticipated outcomes may be.

   b. The IEP process provides an opportunity for resolving any differences between the parents and the agency concerning the special education needs of a child with a disability: first, through the IEP meeting and, second, if necessary, through the procedural protections that are available to the parents.

   c. The IEP sets forth in writing a commitment of resources necessary to enable a child with a disability to receive needed special education and related services.

   d. The IEP is a management tool that is used to ensure that each child with a disability is provided special education and related services appropriate to the child's special learning needs.

   e. The IEP is a compliance/monitoring document that may be used by authorized monitoring personnel from each governmental level to determine whether a child with a disability is actually receiving the FAPE agreed to by the parents and the school.

   f. The IEP serves as an evaluation device for use in determining the extent of the child's progress toward meeting the projected outcomes.

NOTE: The Act does not require that teachers or other school personnel be held accountable if a child with a disability does not achieve the goals and objectives set forth in the IEP.

II.

IEP REQUIREMENTS Q & A

a. Public Agencies

The SEA (State) shall (must) ensure that each public agency develops and implements an IEP for each of its children with disabilities.

b. Private schools and facilities

The SEA shall ensure that an IEP is developed and implemented for each child with a disability who-

(1) Is placed in or referred to a private school or facility by a public agency; or

(2) Is enrolled in a parochial school or other private school and receives special education or related services from a public agency.

NOTE: This section applies to all public agencies, including other State agencies (e.g., departments of mental health and welfare) that provide special education to a child with a disability, either directly, by contract, or through other arrangements. Thus, if a State welfare agency contracts with a private school or facility to provide special education to a child with a disability, that agency would be responsible for ensuring that an IEP is developed for the child.

Q&A

1. *Who is responsible for ensuring the development of IEPs for children with disabilities served by a public agency, other than a local (school)?*

The answer will vary from State to State, depending upon State law, policy, or practice. In each State, however, the SEA is ultimately responsible for ensuring that each agency in the State is in compliance with the IEP requirements and the other provisions of the Act and regulations. The SEA must ensure that every child with a disability in the State has FAPE available, regardless of which agency, State or local, is responsible for the child. While the SEA has flexibility in deciding the best means to meet this obligation (e.g., through interagency agreements), there can be no failure to provide FAPE due to jurisdictional disputes among agencies.

NOTE: The requirements of the Act and regulations apply to all political subdivisions of the State that are involved in the education of children with disabilities, including (1) the SEA, (2) LEAs, (3) other State agencies such as Departments of Mental Health and Welfare, and State schools for students with deafness or students with blindness, and (4) State correctional facilities.

The following paragraphs outline (1) some of the SEA's responsibilities for developing policies or agreements under a variety of interagency situations, and (2) some of the responsibilities of an LEA when it initiates the placement of a child with a disability in a school or program operated by another State agency:

a. SEA policies or interagency agreements

The SEA, through its written policies or agreements, must ensure that IEPs are properly written and implemented for all children with disabilities in the State. This applies to each interagency situation that exists in the State, including any of the following:

(1) When an LEA initiates the placement of a child in a school or program operated by another State agency;

(2) When a State or local agency other than the SEA or LEA places a child in a residential facility or other program;

(3) When parents initiate placements in public institutions; and

(4) When the courts make placements in correctional facilities.

NOTE: This is not an exhaustive list. The SEA's policies must cover any other interagency situation that is applicable in the State, including placements that are made for both educational and non-educational purposes.

Frequently, more than one agency is involved in developing or implementing an IEP of a child with a disability (e.g., when the LEA remains responsible for the child, even though another public agency provides the special education and related services, or when there are shared cost arrangements),. It is important that SEA policies or agreements define the role of each agency involved in the situations described above, in order to resolve any jurisdictional problems that could delay the provision of FAPE to a child with a disability. For example, if a child is placed in a residential facility, any one or all of the following agencies might be involved in the development and/or implementation of the child's IEP. The child's LEA, the SEA, another State agency, an institution or school under that agency, and the LEA where the institution is located.

NOTE: The SEA must also ensure that any agency involved in the education of a child with a disability is in compliance with the LRE provisions of the Act and regulations, and, specifically, with the requirement that the placement of each child with a disability (1) be determined at least annually, (2) be based on the child's IEP, and (3) be as close as possible to the child's home.

b. LEA initiated placements

When an LEA is responsible for the education of a child with a disability, the LEA is also responsible for developing the child's IEP. The LEA has this responsibility even if development of the IEP results in placement in a State-operated school or program.

NOTE: The IEP must be developed before the child is placed. When placement in a State-operated school is necessary, the affected State agency or agencies must be involved by the LEA in the development of the IEP. After the child enters the State school, meetings to review or revise the child's IEP could be conducted by either the LEA or the State school, depending upon State law, policy, or practice. However, both agencies should be involved in any decisions made; (2) is regarded by both the parents and agency as appropriate in terms of the child's needs, about the child's IEP (either by attending the IEP meetings, or through correspondence or telephone calls). There must be a clear decision, based upon State law, as to whether responsibility for the child's education is transferred to the State school or remains with the LEA, since this decision determines which agency is responsible for reviewing or revising the child's IEP.

2. *For a child placed out of State by a public agency, is the placing or receiving State responsible for the child's IEP?*

The "placing" State is responsible for developing the child's IEP and ensuring that it is implemented. The determination of the specific agency in the placing State that is responsible for the child's IEP would be based on State law, policy, or practice. However, as indicated above, the SEA in thee placing State is responsible for ensuring that the child has FAPE available.

3. *When must IEPs be in effect?*

(a) At the beginning of each school year, each public agency shall have in effect an IEP for every child with a disability who is receiving special education from that agency.

(b) An IEP must-

(1) Be in effect before special education and related services are provided to the child; and

(2) Be implemented as soon as possible following the IEP meeting.

NOTE: It is expected that the IEP of a child with a disability will be implemented immediately following the meeting(s). An exception to this would be (1) when the meetings occur during the summer vacation period, or (2) where there are circumstances that require a short delay (e.g., working out transportation arrangements). However, there can be no undue delay in providing special education and related services to the child.

4. *In requiring that an IEP be in effect before special education and related services are provided, what does "be in effect" mean?*

As used in the regulations, the term "be in effect" means that the IEP (1) has been developed properly (i.e., at a meeting(s) involving all of the participants specified in the Act (parent, teacher, agency representative, and, if appropriate, the child), and (2) is regarded by both the parents and agency as appropriate in terms of the child's needs specified goals and objectives, and the services to be provided; and (3) will be implemented as written.

5. *How much of a delay is permissible between the time the IEP of a child with a disability is finalized and when special education is provided?*

In general, no delay is permissible. It is expected that the special education and related services set out in a child's IEP will be provided by the agency beginning immediately after the IEP is finalized...unless otherwise specified in the IEP, services must be provided as soon as possible after the meeting.

6. *For a child with a disability receiving special education for the first time, when must an IEP be developed- before or after placement?*

An IEP must be in effect before special education and related services are provided to the child. The appropriate placement for a given child with a disability cannot be determined until after decisions have been made about what the child's needs are and what will be provided. Since these decisions are made at the IEP meeting, it would not be permissible to first place the child and then develop the IEP. Therefore, the IEP must be developed before placement. The above requirement does not preclude temporarily placing an eligible child with a disability in a program as part of the evaluation process- before the IEP is finalized- to aid in determining the most appropriate placement for the child. It is essential that the temporary placement not become the final placement before the IEP is finalized. In order to ensure this does not happen, the State might consider requiring LEAs to take the following actions:

a. Develop and interim IEP for the child that sets out the specific conditions and timelines for the trial placement.

b. Ensure that the parents agree to the interim placement before it is carried out, and that they are involved throughout the process of developing, reviewing, and revising the child's IEP.

c. Set a specific timeline (e.g.30 days) for completing the evaluation and making judgments about the most appropriate placement for the child.

d. Conduct an IEP meeting at the end of the trial period in order to finalize the child's IEP.

NOTE: Once the IEP of the child with a disability is in effect and the child is placed in a special education program, the teacher might develop detailed lesson plans or objectives based on the IEP. However, these lesson plans and objectives are not required to be a part of the IEP itself.

7. If a child with a disability has been receiving special education in one LEA and moves to another community, must the new LEA hold an IEP meeting before the child is placed in a special education program?

It would not be necessary for the new LEA to conduct an IEP meeting if:

1. A copy of the child's current IEP is available;

2. the parents indicate that they are satisfied with the current IEP; and

3. the new LEA determines that the current IEP is appropriate and can be implemented as written.

If the child's current IEP is not available, or if either the LEA or the parent believes that it is not appropriate, an IEP meeting would have to be conducted. This meeting should take place within a short time after the child enrolls in the new LEA (normally, within one week). If the LEA or the parents believe that additional; information is needed (e.g., the school records from the former LEA) or that a new evaluation is necessary before a final placement decision can be made, it would be permissible to temporarily place the child in an interim program before the IEP is finalized.

8. Meetings

(a) General

Each agency is responsible for initiating and conducting meetings for the purpose of developing, reviewing, and revising the IEP of a child with a disability. A meeting to develop an IEP for a child must be held within 30 calendar days of a determination that the child needs special education and related services. A meeting to review the IEP must be held at least once a year.

NOTE: The date on which agencies must have IEPs in effect is at the beginning of the school year. However, except for new children with disabilities (i.e., those evaluated and determined to need special education and related services for the first time), the timing of meetings to develop, review and revise IEPs is left to the discretion of each agency. In order to have IEPs in effect at the beginning of the school year, agencies could hold meetings either at the end of the preceding school year or during the summer prior to the next school year. Meetings may be held any time throughout the year, as long as IEPs are in effect at the beginning of the school year. The law requires agencies to hold a meeting at least once a year in order to review and, if appropriate, revise each child's IEP. The timing of those meetings could be *on the* anniversary date of the child's last IEP meeting, but this is left to the discretion of the agency.

9. What is the purpose of the 30 day timeline?

The 30 day timeline ensures that there will not be a significant delay between the time a child is evaluated and when the child begins to receive special education. Once it is determined- through the evaluation- that a child has a disability, the public agency has up to 30 days to hold an IEP meeting.

10. Must the agency hold a separate meeting to determine a child's eligibility for special education and related services, or can this step be combined with the IEP meeting?

Rules for evaluation procedures provide that the evaluation of each child with a disability must be "made by a multidisciplinary team or group of persons..." The decisions regarding

(1) whether the team members actually met together, and

(2) whether such meetings are separate from the IEP meeting are matters that are left to the discretion of the State or local agencies.

In practice, some agencies hold separate eligibility meetings with the multidisciplinary team before the IEP meeting. Other agencies combine the two steps into one. If a combined meeting is conducted, the public agency must include the parents as participants at the meeting.

NOTE: When separate meetings are conducted, placement decisions would be made at the IEP meeting. However, placement options could be discussed at the eligibility meeting. If, at a separate eligibility meeting, a decision is made that a child is not eligible for special education, the parents should be notified about the decision.

11. Must IEPs be reviewed or revised at the beginning of each school year?

No. The basic requirement in the regulations is that IEPs must be in effect at the beginning of each school year. Meetings must be conducted at least once each year to review and, if necessary, revise the IEP of each child with a disability. However, the meetings may be held anytime during the year, including

(1) at the end of the school year,
(2) during the summer, before the new school year begins, or
(3) on the anniversary date of the last IEP meeting on the child.

12. *How frequently must IEP meetings be held and how long should they be?*

The Act provides that each public agency must hold meetings periodically, but not less than annually, to review each child's IEP and, if appropriate, revise its provisions. The legislative history of the Act makes it clear that there should be as many meetings a year as any one child may need. There is no prescribed length for IEP meetings. In general, meetings (1) will be longer for initial placements and for children who require a variety of complex services, and (2) will be shorter for continuing placements and for children who require only a minimum amount of services. In any event, however, it is expected that agencies will allow sufficient time at the meetings to ensure meaningful parent participation.

13. *Who can initiate IEP meetings?*

IEP meetings are initiated and conducted at the discretion of the public agency. However, if the parents of a child with a disability believe that the child is not progressing satisfactorily or that there is a problem with the child's current IEP, it would be appropriate for the parents to request an IEP meeting. The public agency should grant any reasonable request for such a meeting. If a child's teacher feels that the child's placement or IEP services are not appropriate to the child, the teacher should follow agency procedures with respect to (1) calling or meeting with the parents and/or (2) requesting the agency to hold another meeting to review the child's IEP.

14. *May IEP meetings be tape-recorded?*

The use of tape recorders at IEP meetings is not addressed by either the Act or the regulations. Although taping is clearly not required, it is permissible at the option of either the parents or the agency. However, if the recording is maintained by the agency, it is an education record and would, therefore, be subject to the confidentiality requirements.

15. *Participants in meetings*
(a) General

The public agency shall ensure that each meeting includes the following participants:
(1) A representative of the public agency, other than the child's teacher, who is qualified to provide, or supervise the provision of special education.
(2) The child's teacher.
(3) One or both of the child's parents,
(4) The child, if appropriate,
(5) Other individuals at the discretion of the parents or agency.

(b) Evaluation Personnel

For a child with a disability who has been evaluated for the first time, the public agency shall ensure-

(1) That a member of the evaluation team participates in the meeting; or
(2) That the representative of the public agency, the child's teacher, or some other person is present at the meeting, who is knowledgeable about the evaluation procedures used with the child and is familiar with the results of the evaluation.

(c) Transition services participants

(1) If a purpose of the meeting is the consideration of transition services for a student, the public agency shall invite-

(i) The student, and
(ii) A representative of any other agency that is likely to be responsible for providing or paying for transition services.

(2) If the student does not attend, the public agency shall take other steps to ensure that the student's preferences and interests are considered, and

(3) If an agency invited to send a representative to a meeting does not do so, the public agency shall take other steps to obtain the participation of the other agency in the planning of any transition services.

NOTE:
1. In deciding which teacher will participate in meetings on a child's IEP, the agency may wish to consider the following possibilities:

a. For a child with a disability who is receiving special education, the teacher could be the child's special education teacher. If the child's disability is a speech impairment, the teacher could be the speech-language pathologist.
b. For a child with a disability who is being considered for placement in special education, the teacher could be the child's regular teacher, or a teacher qualified to provide education in the type of program in which a child may be placed, or both.
c. If the child is not in school or has more than one teacher, the agency may designate which teacher will participate in the meeting. Either the teacher or the agency representative should be qualified in the area of the child's suspected disability.
d. For a child whose primary disability is a speech or language impairment, the evaluation personnel would normally be the one participating. The public agency is required to invite each student to participate in his/her IEP meeting. If a purpose of the meeting is the consideration of transition services for the student. For all students who are 16 years of age or older, one of the purposes of the annual meeting will always be the planning of transition services, since transition services are a required component of the IEP for these students. For a student younger than age 16, if transition services are initially discussed at a meeting that does not include the student, the public agency is responsible for ensuring that, before a decision about transition services for the student is made, a subsequent IEP meeting is conducted for that purpose, and the student is invited to the meeting.

16. *Who can serve as the representative of the public agency at an IEP meeting?*

The representative of the public agency could be any member of the school staff, other than the child's teacher, who is qualified to provide, or supervise the provision of specially designed instruction to meet the unique needs of children with disabilities. Thus, the agency representative could be (1) a qualified special education administrator, supervisor or teacher (including a speech-language pathologist0, or (2) a school principal or other administrator- if the person is qualified to provide or supervise the provision of special education. Each State or local agency may determine which specific staff member will serve as the agency representative. However, the representative should be able to ensure that whatever services are set out in the IEP will actually be provided and that the IEP will not be vetoed at a higher administrative level within the agency. Thus, the person selected should have the authority to commit agency resources (i.e., to make decisions about the specific special education and related services that the agency will provide to a particular child. For a child with a disability who requires only a limited amount of special education, the agency representative able to commit appropriate resources could be a special education teacher. For a child who requires extensive special education and related services, the agency representative might need to be a key administrator in the agency. IEP meetings for continuing placements could be more routine than those for initial placements, and, this, might not require the participation of a key administrator.

17. *Who is the representative of the public agency if a child with a disability is served by a public agency other than the SEA or LEA?*

The answer depends on which agency is responsible, under State law, policy, or practice, for any one or all of the following:

1. The child's education,
2. Placing the child,
3. Providing (or paying for the provision of) special education and related services to the child. In general, the agency representative at the IEP meeting would be a member of the agency or institution that is responsible for the child's education. For example, if a State agency

1. places a child in an institution,
2. is responsible under State law for the child's education, and
3. has a qualified special education staff at the institution, then a member of the institution's staff would be the agency representative at the IEP meetings. Sometimes there is no special education staff at the institution, and the children are served by special education personnel from the LEA where the institution is located. In this situation, a member of the LEA staff would usually serve as the agency representative.

18. *For a child with a disability being considered for initial placement in special education, which teacher should attend the IEP meeting?*

The teacher should be either

1. a teacher qualified to provide special education in the child's area of disability, or
2. the child's regular teacher.

At the option of the agency, both teachers could attend. In any event, there should be at least one member of the school staff at the meeting (e.g., the agency representative or the teacher) who is qualified in the child's area of suspected disability.

NOTE: Sometimes more than one meeting is necessary in order to finalize a child's IEP. If, in this process, the special education teacher who will be working with the child is identified, it would be useful to have that teacher participate in the meeting with the parents and other members of the IEP team in finalizing the IEP. When this is not possible, the agency should ensure that the teacher is given a copy of the child's IEP as soon as possible after the IEP is finalized and before the teacher begins working with the child.

19. *If a child with a disability is enrolled in both regular and special education classes, which teacher should attend the IEP meeting?*

In general, the teacher at the IEP meeting should be the child's special education teacher. At the option of the agency or the parent, the child's regular teacher also might attend. If the regular teacher does not attend, the agency should either provide the regular teacher with a copy of the IEP or inform the regular teacher of its contents. Moreover, the agency should ensure that the special education teacher, or other appropriate support person, is able, as necessary, to consult with and be a resource to the child's regular teacher.

20. *If a child with a disability in high school attends several regular classes, must all of the child's regular teachers attend the IEP meeting?*

No. Only one teacher must attend. However, at the option of the LEA, additional teachers of the child may attend. The following points should be considered in making this decision:

a. Generally, the number of participants at an IEP meeting should be small. Small meetings have several advantages over large ones. For example, they (1) allow for more open, active parent involvement, (2) are less costly, (3) are easier to arrange and conduct, and (4) are usually more productive.

b. While large meetings are generally inappropriate, there may be specific circumstances where the participation of additional staff would be beneficial. When the participation of the regular teachers is considered by the agency or the parents to be beneficial to the child's success in school ,(e.g., in terms of the child's participation in the regular education program), it would be appropriate for them to attend the meeting.

c. Although the child's regular teachers would not routinely attend IEP meetings, they would either (1) be informed about the child's IEP by the special education teacher or agency representative, and/or (2) receive a copy of the IEP itself.

21. *If a child's primary disability is a speech impairment, must the child's regular teacher attend the IEP meeting?*
No. A speech-language pathologist would usually serve as the child's teacher for purposes of the IERP meeting. The regular teacher could also attend at the option of the school.

22. *If a child is enrolled in a special education class because of a primary disability, and also receives speech-language pathology services, must both specialists attend the meeting?*

No. It is not required that both attend. The special education teacher would attend the meeting as the child's teacher. The speech-language pathologist could either (1) participate in the meeting itself, (2) provide a written recommendation concerning the nature, frequency, and amount of services to be provided to the child.

23. *When may representatives of teacher organizations attend IEP meetings?*

Officials of teacher organizations may not attend IEP meetings if personally identifiable information from the student's education records is discussed- except with the prior written consent of the parents. In addition, the law does not provide for the participation of representatives of teacher organizations at IEP meetings. The legislative history of the Act makes it clear that attendance at IEP meetings should be limited to those who have an intense interest in the child. Since a representative of a teacher organization would be concerned with the interests of the teacher rather than the interests of the child, it would be inappropriate for such an official to attend an IEP meeting.

24. *When may a child with a disability attend an IEP meeting?*

Generally, a child with a disability should attend the IEP meeting whenever the parent decides that it is appropriate for the child to do so. Whenever possible, the agency and parents should discuss the appropriateness of the child's participation before a decision is made, in order to help the parents determine whether or not the child's attendance will be (I1) helpful in developing the IEP and/or (2) directly beneficial to the child. The agency should inform the parents before each IEP meeting that they may invite their child to participate.

NOTE: The parents and agency should encourage older children with disabilities, particularly those at the secondary school level, to participate in their IERP meetings.

25. *Do the parents of a student with a disability retain the right to attend the IEP meeting when the student reaches the age of majority?*

The Act is silent concerning any modification of the rights of the parents of a student with a disability when the student reaches the age of majority.

26. *Must related services personnel attend IEP meetings?*

No. It is not required that they attend. However, if a child with a disability has an identified need for related services, it would be appropriate for the related services personnel to attend the meeting or otherwise be involved in developing the IEP. For example, when the child's evaluation indicates the need for a specific related service (e.g., physical therapy, occupational therapy, or counseling) the agency should ensure that a qualified provider of that service either (1) attends the IEP meeting, or (2) provides a written recommendation concerning the nature, frequency and amount of service to be provided to the child.

27. *Are agencies required to use a case manager in the development of the IEP of a child with a disability?*

No. However, some agencies have found it helpful to have a special educator or some other school staff member (e.g., a social worker, counselor, or psychologist) serve as coordinator or case manager of the IEP process for an individual child or for all children with disabilities served by the agency. Examples of the kinds of activities that case managers might carry out are: (1) coordinating the multidisciplinary evaluation; (2) collecting and synthesizing the evaluation reports and other relevant information about a child that might be needed at the IEP meeting, (3) communicating with the parents; and (4) participating in, or conducting the IEP meeting itself.

28. *For a child with a speech impairment, who must represent the evaluation team at the IEP meeting?*

No specific person must represent the evaluation team. However, a speech-language pathologist would normally be the most appropriate representative. For many children whose primary disability is speech impairment, there may be no other evaluation personnel involved. Children who have a speech impairment as their primary disability may not need a complete battery of assessments (e.g., psychological, physical, or adaptive behavior). However, a qualified speech-language pathologist would (1) evaluate each child with a speech impairment using procedures that are appropriate for the diagnosis and appraisal of speech and language impairments, and (2) if necessary, make referrals for additional assessments needed to make an appropriate placement decision.

Parent participation

(a) Each public agency shall take steps to ensure that one or both of the parents of the child with a disability are present at each meeting or are afforded the opportunity to participate, including-

(1) Notifying parents of the meeting early enough to ensure that they will have an opportunity to attend, and

(2) Scheduling the meeting at a mutually agreed upon time and place.

(b) (1) The notice about the meeting must indicate the purpose, time, and location of the meeting and who will be in attendance.

(2) If a purpose of the meeting is the consideration of transition services for a student, the notice must also-
  (i) Indicate the purpose;
  (ii) Indicate that the agency will invite the student; and
  (iii) Identify any other agency that will be invited to send a representative.

(c) If neither parent can attend, the public agency shall use other methods to ensure parent participation, including individual or conference telephone calls.

(d) A meeting may be conducted without a parent in attendance if the public agency is unable to convince the parents that they should attend. In this case the public agency must have a record of its attempts to arrange a mutually agreed upon time and place such as-
  (1) Detailed records of telephone calls made or attempted and the results of those calls;
  (2) Copies of correspondence sent to the parents and any responses received; and
  (3) Detailed records of visits made to the parent's home or place of employment and the results of those visits.
 (e) The Public agency shall take whatever action is necessary to ensure that the parent understands the proceedings at a meeting, including arranging for an interpreter for parents with deafness or whose native language is other than English.

(f) The public agency shall give the parent, on request, a copy of the IEP.

NOTE: Notice of the meeting could also inform parents that they may bring other people to the meeting.

29. *What is the role of the parents at the IEP meeting?*

The parents of a child with a disability are expected to be equal participants along with school personnel, in developing, reviewing, and revising the child's IEP. This is an active role in which parents (1) participate in the discussion about the child's need for special education and related services, and (2) join with the other participants in deciding what services the agency will provide to the child.

NOTE: In some instances, parents might elect to bring another participant to the meeting, e.g., a friend, a neighbor, someone outside of the agency who is familiar with applicable laws and with the child's needs, or a specialist who conducted an independent evaluation of the child.

30. *What is the role of a surrogate parent at an IEP meeting?*

A surrogate parent is a person appointed to represent the interests of a child with a disability in the education decision-making process when that child has no other parent representation. The surrogate has all of the rights and responsibilities of the parents. This, they are entitled to (1) participate in the child's IEP meeting, (2) see the child's education records, and (3) receive notice, grant consent, and invoke due process to resolve differences.

31. *Must the public agency let the parents know who will be at the IEP meeting?*

Yes. In notifying parents about the meeting, the agency "must indicate the purpose, time, and location of the meeting, and who will be in attendance." If possible, the agency should give the name and position of each person who will attend. In addition, the agency should inform the parents of their right to bring other participants to the meeting. It is also appropriate for the agency to ask whether the parents intend to bring a participant to the meeting.

32. *Are parents required to sign IEPs?*

Parent signatures are not required by either the Act or regulations. However, having such signatures is considered by parents, advocates, and public agency personnel to be useful. The following are some of the ways that IEPs signed by parents and/or agency personnel might be used:

(a) A signed IEP is one way to document who attended the meeting. If signatures are not used, the agency must document attendance in some other way.
(b) An IEP signed by the parents is one way to indicate that the parents approved the child's special education program.

NOTE: If, after signing, the parents feel that a change is needed in the IEP, it would be appropriate for them to request another meeting.

(2) An IEP signed by an agency representative provides the parents with a signed record of the services that the agency has agreed to provide. Even if the school personnel do not sign, the agency still must provide, or ensure the provision of the services called for in the IEP.

33. *If the parent signs the IEP, does the signature indicate consent for initial placement?*

The parent's signature on the IEP would satisfy the consent requirement concerning initial placement of the child only if the IEP includes a statement on initial placement that meets the definition of consent. Consent means that:
(a) The parent has been fully informed of all information relevant to the activity for which consent is sought;
(b) The parent understands and agrees in writing to the carrying out of the activity for which his or her consent is sought, and the consent describes that activity and lists the records, if any, that will be released and to whom; and

(c) The parent understands that the granting of consent is voluntary and may be revoked at any time.

34. Do parents have the right to a copy of their child's IEP?

Yes. The public agency shall give the parent, on request, a copy of the IEP. In order that parents may know about this provision, it is recommended that they be informed about it at the IEP meeting and/or receive a copy of the IEP itself within a reasonable time following the meeting.

35. *Must parents be informed at the IEP meeting of their right to appeal?*

If the agency has already informed the parent of their right to appeal, as is required, it would not be necessary for the agency to do this again at the IEP meeting. Written notice must give the parents a reasonable time before the public agency proposes or refuses "to initiate or change the identification, evaluation, or educational placement of the child or the provision of FAPE to the child." Notice must provide a full explanation of all of the procedural safeguards available to the parents. The IEP meeting serves as a communication vehicle between parents and school personnel, and enables them, as equal participants, to jointly decide upon what the child's needs are, what will be provided, and what the anticipated outcomes may be. If, during the IEP meeting, parents and school staff are unable to reach agreement, the agency should remind the parents that they may seek to resolve their differences through the due process procedures. Either a parent or a public educational agency may initiate a hearing on any matter. Every effort should be made to resolve differences between parents and school staff without resort to a due process hearing (i.e., through voluntary mediation or some other informal step). However, mediation or other informal procedures may not be used to deny or delay a parent's right to a due process hearing.

36. *Does the IEP include ways for parents to check the progress of their children?*

In general, the answer is yes. The IEP document is a written record of decisions jointly made by parents and school personnel at the IEP meeting regarding the special education program of a child with a disability. That record includes agreed upon items, such as goals and objectives, and the specific special education and related services to be provided to the child. The goals and objectives in the IEP should be helpful to both parents and school personnel, in a general way, in checking on a child's progress in the special education program. However, since the IEP is not intended to include the specifics about a child's total educational program that are found in daily, weekly, or monthly instructional plans, parents will often need to obtain more specific, on-going information about the child's progress- through parent-teacher conferences, report cards and other reporting procedures ordinarily used by the agency.

37. *Must IEPs include specific checkpoint intervals for parents to confer with teachers and to revise or update their children's IEP?*

No. The IEP of a child with a disability is not required to include specific "checkpoint intervals" (i.e., meeting dates) for reviewing the child's progress. However, in individual situations, specific meeting dates could be designated in the IEP, if the parents and school personnel believe that it would be helpful to do so. Although meeting dates are not required to be set out in the IEP itself, there are specific provisions in the regulations and in this document regarding agency responsibilities in initiating IEP meetings, including the following:

1. Public agencies must hold meetings periodically, but not less than annually, to review, and if appropriate, revise each child's IEP;
2. There should be as many meetings a year as the child needs; and
3. Agencies should grant any reasonable parental request for an IEP meeting.

In addition to the above provisions, it is expected that, through an agency's general reporting procedures for all children in school, there will be specific designated times for parents to review their child's progress (e.g., through periodic parent-teacher conferences and/or the use of report cards, letters, or other reporting devices.)

38. *If the parents and agency are unable to reach agreement at an IEP meeting, what steps should be followed until agreement is reached?*

As a general rule, the agency and parents would agree to an interim course of action for serving the child (i.e., in terms of placement and/or services) to be followed until the area of disagreement over the IEP is resolved. The manner in which this interim measure is developed and agreed to by both parties is left to the discretion of the individual State or local agency. However, if the parents and agency cannot agree on an interim measure, the child's last agreed upon IEP would remain in effect in the areas of disagreement until the disagreement is resolved. The following may be helpful to agencies if there are disagreements:

a. There may be instances where the parents and agency are in agreement about the basic IEP services (e.g., the child's placement and/or the special education services), but disagree about the provision of a particular related service (i.e., whether the service is needed and/or the amount to be provided). In such cases, it is recommended (1) that the IEP be implemented in all areas where there is agreement, (2) that the document indicate the points of disagreement, and (3) that procedures be initiated to resolve the disagreement.
b. Sometimes the disagreement is with the placement or kind of special education to be provided (e.g., one party proposes a self-contained placement, and the other proposes resource room services). In such cases, the agency might, for example, carry out any one or all of the following steps:

1. Remind the parents that they may resolve their differences through the due process procedures;
2. Work with parents to develop an interim course of action (in terms of placement and/or services) that
    both parties can agree to until resolution is reached; and

3. Recommend the use of mediation or some other informal procedure for resolving the differences without going to a due process hearing.

c. If, because of the disagreement over the IEP, a hearing is initiated by either the parent or the agency, the agency may not change the child's placement unless the parents and agency agree otherwise. The following two examples are related to this requirement:

1. A child in the regular fourth grade has been evaluated and found to be eligible for special education. The agency and parents agree that the child has a specific learning disability. However, one party proposes placement in a self-contained program, and the other proposes placement in a resource room. Agreement cannot be reached and a due process hearing is initiated. Unless the parents and agency agree otherwise, the child would remain in the regular fourth grade until the issue is resolved. On the other hand, since the child's need for special education is not in question, both parties might agree- as an interim measure- (1) to temporarily place the child in either one of the programs proposed at the meeting, or (2) to serve the child through some other temporary arrangement.

2. A child with a disability is currently receiving special education under an existing IEP. A due process hearing has been initiated regarding an alternative special education placement for the child. Unless the parents and agency agree otherwise, the child would remain in the current placement. In this situation, the child's IEP could be revised, as necessary, and implemented in all of the areas agreed to by the parents and agency, while the area of disagreement is being settled through due process.

NOTE: If the due process hearing concerns whether or not a particular service should continue to be provided under the IEP (e.g., physical therapy), that service would continue to be provided to the child under the IEP that was in effect at the time the hearing was initiated (1) unless the parents and agency agree to a change in the services, or (2) until the issue is resolved.

Content of the Individualized Education Program

(a) General
The IEP for each child must include-

1. A statement of the child's present levels of educational performance;
2. A statement of annual goals, including short-term instructional objectives;
3. A statement of the specific special education and related services to be provided to the child and the extent that the child will be able to participate in the regular educational program;
4. The projected dates for initiation of services and the anticipated duration of the services;
5. Appropriate objective criteria and evaluation procedures and schedules for determining, on at least an annual basis, whether the short term instructional objectives are being achieved.

(b) Transition services

1. The IEP for each student, beginning no later than age 16 (and at a younger age if determined appropriate) must include a statement of the needed transition services, including, if appropriate, a statement of each public agency and each participating agency's responsibilities or linkages, or both, before the student leaves the school setting;

2. If the IEP team determines that services are not needed in one or more of the required areas, the IEP must include a statement to that effect and the basis upon which the statement was made.

NOTE: The legislative history of the transition services provisions of the Act suggests that the statement of needed transition services should include a commitment by any participating agency to meet any financial responsibility it may have in the provision of transition services... The Act provides that IEPs must include the provision of these services and a statement of needed transition services for students beginning no later than age 16, but permits transition services to students below age 16. Although the statute does not mandate transition services for all students beginning at age 14 or younger, the provision of these services could have a significantly positive effect on the employment and independent living outcomes for many of these students in the future, especially for students who are likely to drop out before age 16. Congress expects consideration to be given to the need for transition services for some students by age 14 or younger. It encourages that approach because of concern that age 16 may be too late for many students, particularly those at risk of dropping out of school and those with the most severe disabilities. Even for those students who stay in school until age 18, many will need more than two years of transition services. Students with disabilities are now dropping out of school before age 18 feeling that the education system has little to offer them. Initiating services at a younger age will be critical.

39. *What should be included in the statement of the child's present levels of educational performance?*

The statement of present levels of educational performance will be different for each child with a disability. Determinations about the content of the statement for an individual child are matters that are left to the discretion of participants in the IEP meetings. However, the following are some points that should be taken into account in writing this part of the IEP:

(a) The statement should accurately describe the effect of the child's disability on the child's performance in any area of education that is affected, including

(1) academic areas (reading, math, communication, etc.), and
(2) non-academic areas (daily life activities, mobility, etc.)

NOTE: Labels such as mental retardation of deafness may not be used as a substitute for the description of present levels of functioning.

(b) The statement should be written in objective, measureable terms, to the extent possible. Data from the child's evaluation would be a good source of such information. Test scores that are pertinent to the child's diagnosis might be included, if appropriate. However, the scores should be (1) self-explanatory (i.e., they can be interpreted by all participants without the use of test manuals or other aids), or (2) an explanation should be included. Whatever test results are used should reflect the impact of the disability on the child's performance. Thus, raw scores would not usually be sufficient.

(c) There should be a direct relationship between the present levels of educational performance and the other components of the IEP. Thus, if the statement describes a problem with the child's reading level and points to a deficiency in a specific reading skill, this problem should be addressed under both (1) goals and objectives, and (2) specific special education and related services to be provided to the child.

40. *Why are goals and objectives required in the IEP?*

The statutory requirements for including annual goals and short term instructional objectives, and for having at least an annual review of the IEP of a child with a disability provide a mechanism for determining (1) whether the anticipated outcomes for the child are being met (i.e., whether the child is progressing in the special education program), and (2) whether the placement and services are appropriate to the child's special learning needs. In effect, these requirements provide a way
for the child's teachers and parents to be able to track the child's progress in special education. However, the goals and objectives in the IEP are not intended to be as specific as the goals and objectives that are normally found in daily, weekly, or monthly instructional plans.

41. *What are annual goals in an IEP?*

The annual goals in the IEP are statements that describe what a child with a disability can reasonably be expected to accomplish within a 12 month period in the child's special education program. There should be a direct relationship between the annual goals and the present levels of educational performance.

42. *What are short term instructional objectives in an IEP?*

Short term instructional objectives are measureable, intermediate steps between the present levels of educational performance of a child with a disability and the annual goals that are established for the child. The objectives are developed based on a logical breakdown of the major components of the annual goals and can serve as milestones for measuring progress toward meeting the goals. In some respects, IEP objectives are similar to objectives used in daily classroom instructional plans. For example, both kinds of objectives are used (1) to describe what a given child is expected to accomplish in a particular area within some specified time period, and (2) to determine the extent that the child is progressing toward those accomplishments.

On other respects, objectives in IEPs are different from those used in instructional plans, primarily in the amount of detail they provide. IEP objectives provide general benchmarks for determining progress toward meeting the annual goals. These objectives should be projected to be accomplished on a daily, weekly, or monthly basis. Classroom instructional plans generally include details not required in an IEP, such as specific methods, activities, and materials (e.g., use of flash cards) that will be used in accomplishing the objectives.

43. *Should the IEP goals and objectives focus only on special education and related services, or should they relate to the total education of the child?*
IEP goals and objectives are concerned primarily with meeting the needs of a child with a disability for special education and related services, and are not required to cover other areas of the child's education. Stated another way, the goals and objectives in the IEP should focus on offsetting or reducing the problems resulting from the child's disability that interfere with learning and educational performance in school. For example, if a child with a learning disability is functioning several grades below the child's indicated ability in reading and has a specific problem with word recognition, the IEP goals and objectives would be directed toward (1) closing the gap between the child's indicated ability and current level of functioning, and (2) helping the child increase the ability to use word attack skills, by effectively (or to find some other approach to increase independence in reading).

For a child with a mild speech impairment, the IEP objectives would focus on improving the child's communication skills, by either (1) correcting the impairment, or (2) minimizing its effect on the child's ability to communicate. On the other hand, the goals and objectives for a child with severe mental retardation would be more comprehensive and cover more of the child's school program than if the child has only a mild disability.

44. *Should there be a relationship between the goals and objectives in the IEP and those that are in instructional plans of special education personnel?*

Yes. There should be a direct relationship between the IEP goals and objectives for a given child with a disability and the goals and objectives that are in the special education instructional plans for the child. However, the IEP is not intended to be detailed enough to be used as an instructional plan. The IEP, through its goals and objectives, (1) sets the general direction to be taken by those who will implement the IEP, and (2) serves as the basis for developing a detailed instructional plan for the child.

45. *When must IEP objectives be written- before or after placement?*

IEP objectives must be written before placement. Once a child with a disability is placed in a special education program, the teacher might develop lesson plans or more detailed objectives based on the IEP; however, such plans and objectives are not required to be part of the IEP itself.

46. *Can short term instructional objectives be changed without initiating another IEP meeting?*

No. The agency "is responsible for initiating and conducting meetings for the purpose of developing, reviewing, and revising the IEP of a child with a disability". Since a change in short term instructional objectives constitutes a revision of the child's IEP, the agency must (1) notify the parents of the proposed change; and (2) Initiate an IEP meeting If the parents are unable or unwilling to attend such a meeting, their participation in the revision of the IERP objectives can be obtained through other means, including individual or conference telephone calls.

47. Must the IEP include all special education and related services needed by the child or only those available from the public agency?

Each public agency must provide FAPE to all children with disabilities. Therefore, the IEP for a child with a disability must include all of the specific special education and related services needed by the child- as determined by the child's current evaluation. This means that the services must be listed in the IEP even if they are not directly available from the local agency, and must be provided by the agency through contract or other arrangement.

48. *Is the IEP a commitment to provide services- i.e., must a public agency provide all of the services listed in the IEP?*

Yes. The IEP of each child with a disability must include all services necessary to meet the child's identified special education and related service needs; and all services in the IEP must be provided in order for the agency to be in compliance with the Act.

49. *Must the public agency itself directly provide the services set out in the IEP?*

The public agency responsible for the education of the child with a disability could provide IEP services to the child (1) directly, through the agency's own staff resources, or (2) indirectly, by contracting with another public or private agency, or through other arrangements. In providing the services, the agency may use whatever State, local, Federal, and private sources of support available for those purposes. However, the services must be at no cost to the parents, and responsibility for ensuring that the IEP services are provided remains with the public agency.

50. *Does the IEP include only special education and related services and the extent that the child can participate in regular education programs?*

For some children with disabilities, the IEP will only address a very limited part of their education (e.g., for a child with a speech impairment, the IEP would generally be limited to the child's speech impairment). For other children (e.g., those with profound mental retardation), the IEP might cover their total education. An IEP for a child with a physical disability with no mental or emotional disability, the IEP might cover most of the child's education.

51. *If modifications are necessary for a child with a disability to participate in a regular education program, must they be included in the IEP?*

Yes. If modifications (supplementary aids and services) to the regular education program are necessary to ensure the child's participation in that program, those modifications must be described in the child's IEP (e.g., for a child with a hearing impairment, special seating arrangements or the provision of assignments sin writing). This applies to any regular education program in which the student may participate, including physical education, art, music, and vocational education.

52. *When must physical education (PE) be described or referred to in the IEP?*
PE services must be made available to every child with a disability receiving FAPE. The following paragraphs (1) set out some of the different PE program arrangements for students with disabilities, and (2) indicate whether, and to what extent, PE must be described or referred to in an IEP.

a. Regular PE with nondisabled students

If a student with a disability can participate fully in the regular PE program without any special modifications to compensate for the student's disability, it would not be necessary to describe or refer to PE in the IEP. On the other hand, if some modifications to the regular PE program are necessary for the student to be able to participate in that program, those modifications must be described in the IEP.

b. Specially designed PE

If a student with a disability needs a specially designed PE program, that program must be addressed in all applicable areas of the IEP (e.g., present levels of educational performance, goals and objectives, and services to be provided). However, these statements would not have to be presented in any more detail than the other special education services included in the student's IEP.

c. PE in separate facilities

If a student with a disability is educated in a separate facility, the PE program for that student must be described or referred to in the IEP. However, the kind and amount of information to be included in the IEP would depend on the physical-motor needs of the student and the type of PE program that is to be provided. Thus, if a student is in a separate facility that has a standard PE program (e.g., a residential school for students with deafness), and if it is determined- on the basis of the student's most recent evaluation- that the student is able to participate in that program without any modifications, then the IEP need only note such participation. On the other hand, if special modifications to the PE program are needed for the student to participate, those modifications must be described in the IEP. Moreover, if the student needs an individually designed PE program, that program must be addressed under all applicable parts of the IEP.

53. *If a student with a disability is to receive vocational education, must it be described or referred to in the student's IEP?*

The answer depends on the kind of vocational education program to be provided. If a student with a disability is able to participate in the regular vocational education program without any modifications to compensate for the student's disability, it would not be necessary to include vocational education in the student's IEP. On the other hand, if modifications to the regular vocational education program are necessary in order for the student to participate in that program, those modifications must be included in the IEP. Moreover, if the student needs a specially designed vocational education program, then vocational education must be described in all applicable areas of the student's IEP. However, these statements would not have to be presented in any more detail than the other special education services included in the IEP.

54. *Must the IEP specify the amount of services or may it simply list the services to be provided?*

The amount of services to be provided must be stated in the IEP, so that the level of the agency's commitment of resources will be clear to parents and other IEP team members. The amount of time to be committed to each of the various services to be provided must be (1) appropriate to that specific service, and (2) stated in the IEP in a manner that is clear to all who are involved in both the development and implementation of the IEP. Changes in the amount of services listed in the IEP cannot be made without holding another IEP meeting. However, as long as there is no change in the overall amount, some adjustments in scheduling the services should be possible (based on the professional judgment of the service provider) without holding another IEP meeting.

55. *Must the IEP of a child with a disability indicate the extent that the child will be educated in the regular educational program?*

Yes. The IEP for each child with a disability must include a "statement of...the extent that the child will be able to participate in regular education programs." One way of meeting this requirement is to indicate the percent of time the child will be spending in the regular education program with nondisabled students. Another way is to list the specific regular education classes the child will be attending.

NOTE: If a child with a severe disability, for example, is expected to be in an special classroom setting most of the time, it is recommended that, in meeting the above requirement, the IEP include any non-curricular activities in which the child will be participating with nondisabled students (e.g., lunch, assembly periods, club activities and other special events).

56. *Can the anticipated duration of services be for more than twelve months?*

In general, the anticipated duration of services would be up to twelve months. There is a direct relationship between the anticipated duration of services and the other parts of the IEP (e.g., annual goals and short term instructional objectives), and each part of the IEP would be addressed whenever there is a review of the child's program. If it is anticipated that the child will need a particular service for more than one year, the duration of that service could be projected beyond that time in the IEP. However, the duration of each service must be reconsidered whenever the IEP is reviewed.

57. *Must the evaluation procedures and schedules be included as a separate item in the IEP?*

No. The evaluation procedures and schedules need not be included as a separate item in the IEP, but they must be presented in a recognizable form and be clearly linked to the short term instructional objectives. In many instances, these components are incorporated directly into the objectives.

58. *Is it permissible for an agency to have the IEP completed when the IEP meeting begins?*

No. It is not permissible for an agency to present a completed IEP to parents for their approval before there has been a full discussion with the parents of (1) the child's need for special education and related services, and (2) what services the agency will provide to the child.

59. *Is the IEP a performance contract?*

No. The IEP is not a performance contract that imposes liability on a teacher or public agency if a child with a disability does not meet the IEP objectives. While the agency must provide special education and related services in accordance with the IEP of each child with a disability, the Act does not require that the agency, the teacher, or other persons be held accountable if the child does not achieve the growth projected in the written statement.

ABOUT THE AUTHOR

Marilyn Arons has been a teacher of various subjects and with all grades and ages since 1961.She founded the first parent information center in the United States in 1976, the Parent Information Center of New Jersey, which endured until 2007. This was never funded by either the State or federal government because of having a litigation component. She began the advocacy movement in special education that led to the development of nonlawyer practice in due process hearings, representing approximately 20,000 children and their families during this period. Her expertise and track record in litigation created controversy and federal litigation regarding the unauthorized practice of law and the ability of a nonlawyer to be paid as a consultant. She created the first parent training programs on all aspects of P.L. 94-142 in five states, New Jersey, New York, Pennsylvania, Delaware, and Florida, from the late 1970s until 2002. Central to these programs was examination of the IEP process and the IEP product. Her book, The Nonlawyer Lady (2014), documents this work. She is recognized as a leading national expert in the field of special education.

In 2001, Mrs. Arons founded the Melody Arons Center for Applied Preschool Research and Education, Inc. (MAC), a nonprofit organization. MAC was created as a memorial for her daughter, Melody, who died in 1997. Its purpose was to provide services and research into the nature and needs of preschool children with disabilities. It applied neuroscience principles to child development, with emphasis on sensory integration and music in early intervention and preschool education. MAC has provided services to approximately 150 children since the organization was founded, and written extensively on its methods and outcomes. It continues to the present time.

Mrs. Arons has a degree in music education from Alma College, completed course work for an experimental program at Teachers College in Neuroscience and Education, and received an M.S. in Special Education from Bank Street College. She is licensed as a special education teacher in the State of New York.

In addition to special education, she is also a working musician, performing one concert a year. Other interests are cooking and gardening. Her husband is Raymond Arons, Dr. P.H., with whom she has written several papers. Her son, Jonathan, is an active musician and entertainer who performs throughout the world. She continues her work with preschool children to the present time.

Made in the USA
Middletown, DE
13 November 2017